E-MOTIONAL BUSINESS

FT.com
FINANCIAL TIMES

BOOKS FOR THE FUTURE MINDED

WELCOME TO LIFE AND WORK IN THE DIGITAL ECONOMY

THERE IS A NEW WORLD WHICH WE CAN LOOK AT BUT WE CANNOT SEE. YET WITHIN IT, THE FORCES OF TECHNOLOGY AND IMAGINATION ARE OVERTURNING THE WAY WE WORK AND THE WAY WE DO BUSINESS. FT.COM BOOKS ARE BOTH GATEWAY AND GUIDE TO THIS WORLD. WE UNDERSTAND IT BECAUSE WE ARE PART OF IT. BUT WE ALSO UNDERSTAND THE NEEDS OF BUSINESSES WHICH ARE TAKING THEIR FIRST STEPS INTO IT, AND THOSE STILL STANDING HESITANTLY ON THE THRESHOLD. ABOVE ALL, WE UNDERSTAND THAT, AS WITH ALL BUSINESS CHALLENGES, THE KEY TO SUCCESS LIES NOT WITH THE TECHNOLOGY ITSELF, BUT WITH THE PEOPLE WHO MUST USE IT AND MANAGE IT. PEOPLE LIKE YOU.

LET'S MAKE TECHNOLOGY EVERYBODY'S BUSINESS.

SEE A WORLD OF BUSINESS. VISIT US AT **WWW.FT.COM** TODAY.

IN THE
E WORLD

NO ONE
CAN HEAR YOU
LISTEN...

E-MOTIONAL BUSINESS
NICOLA PHILLIPS

PEARSON EDUCATION LIMITED

HEAD OFFICE:
EDINBURGH GATE
HARLOW CM20 2JE
TEL: +44 (0)1279 623623
FAX: +44 (0)1279 431059

LONDON OFFICE:
128 LONG ACRE
LONDON WC2E 9AN
TEL: +44 (0)20 7447 2000
FAX: +44 (0)20 7240 5771
WEBSITE: WWW.BUSINESS-MINDS.COM

FIRST PUBLISHED IN GREAT BRITAIN IN 2000

ISBN 0 273 65019 X

BRITISH LIBRARY CATALOGUING IN PUBLICATION DATA
A CIP CATALOGUE RECORD FOR THIS BOOK CAN BE OBTAINED FROM THE BRITISH LIBRARY

10 9 8 7 6 5 4 3 2 1

DESIGNED AND TYPESET BY HEAT
PRINTED AND BOUND BY ASHFORD COLOUR PRESS, HAMPSHIRE

THE PUBLISHERS' POLICY IS TO USE PAPER MANUFACTURED FROM SUSTAINABLE FORESTS.

ACKNOWLEDGEMENTS
BILL FOR TRUSTING IN ME, AND KAREN FOR BIG TIME SOULFULNESS.
DOE AND JED FOR BEING CREATIVE ICONS, FROM THE INSIDE OUT....
AS EVER, DEE AND AL FOR CARE AND WARMTH.
KT AND LAURA FOR THE TRUTH, THE BIZARRE AND THE EDGE.
HILARY AND PADDY FOR EXQUISITE INTELLECTUAL/ORAL EDIFICATION AND GRATIFICATION.
HELEN FOR PROVIDING SUCH GREAT SPACE AND MILK.
CHRIS RILEY AND SANDY PARKERSON AT WIEDEN AND KENNEDY.
RANDY NELSON AND PIXAR AND REBECCA.
ANDY FOR SAVING AND SEEING IT, IN MORE WAYS THAN ONE.
SARA FOR SARA.
PJ FOR PJ.
JERI-SAN, ARIGATO, SENSEI.
JAG FOR BELIEVING, DISTRACTING, TECHNICALS, CHOCOLATE AND BEING THERE.
THE USUAL SUSPECTS:
DON MICHAEL.
LYNN AND RICHARD WITHOUT WHOM I WOULDN'T BE GEOGRAPHICALLY HERE.
AM, ROMESH AND KEVIN FOR INTUITION, ECONOMIC CRICKET AND 24TH CENTURY HOOSIER LOVE.
RICHARD, THE SMARTEST AND MOST CLUED UP PUBLISHER AND RED BLOB IN THIS AS OPPOSED TO PARALLEL
UNIVERSES [APART FROM KEVIN OF COURSE], YOU ARE ONE OF THE FEW PEOPLE ON THE PLANET WHO HEARS
ONLINE. YOU BOTH RULE...
AS FOR THE GUYS ON HEAT: INSPIRATIONAL AND INSPIRED JUST AREN'T ADEQUATE. SEE YOU ON THE BEACH.
LINDA, WHO MAKES LIFE POSSIBLE.

THIS BOOK IS FOR LAUREN, WHOSE CONSTANTLY CHANGING CONNECTION WITH ME AND HER WORLD
INSPIRES AND TEACHES ME. YOU WILL ALWAYS BE THE GROUNDING RELATIONSHIP IN MY WORLD.

"BECAUSE UNLESS YOU BELIEVE THAT
THE FUTURE CAN BE BETTER,
IT'S UNLIKELY YOU WILL STEP UP AND TAKE RESPONSIBILITY FOR MAKING IT SO.

IF YOU ASSUME THAT THERE'S NO HOPE,
YOU GUARANTEE THAT THERE WILL BE NO HOPE.

IF YOU ASSUME THAT THERE IS
AN INSTINCT FOR FREEDOM, THERE ARE
OPPORTUNITIES TO CHANGE THINGS, THERE'S A CHANCE YOU MAY CONTRIBUTE
TO MAKING A BETTER WORLD.

THE CHOICE IS YOURS."

[NOAM CHOMSKY]

"IT'S ONLY THE FUTURE..."

TECHNOLOGY IS CHANGING FASTER THAN MARKETS,
MARKETS ARE CHANGING FASTER THAN CUSTOMERS,
CUSTOMERS ARE CHANGING FASTER THAN ORGANIZATIONS,
AND ORGANIZATIONS ARE CHANGING FASTER THAN THE PEOPLE WHO RUN THEM.

CATCH UP.

E-MOTIONAL BUSINESS
RANDOM BEGINNINGS IN A RANDOM WORLD

Humans. Technology. *How do they co-exist?* As much as technology has impacted and changed our lives, our fundamental "human nature" has not changed much, and may not change in the next millennium. The technology of the E world is less important than how we relate to it and each other. *Is this the Age of Technology or the Age of Living Differently?*

ALL HUMANS
  LAUGH
    CRY
      WANT APPROVAL/ACKNOWLEDGEMENT
       DIE

1

Living in the E world changes none of this. It affects the Pace at which we move, the way we spend our Time, the Space we choose to be in, and the Depth of the relationships we have. Business in the E world may be faster, and it is currently conducted by humans with humans. *So how has it affected the way we think about, and behave towards, each other?*

"THE INTERNET MOVES A WALL ON WHAT PEOPLE THINK THEY NEED."
[K.T. MILLER]

This need is in every sphere of your lives, from shopping and mobile phones to sex. This book is about observing where that wall is, offering explanations about why it happens and its impact on your comfort, satisfaction and contentment. *How often have you in the last year thought about something you wanted, gone straight to a website and ordered it, without thinking of the consequences? Will you confess to late sessions on Amazon.com? How necessary are fifty per cent of your calls on your cell phone?* You will undoubtedly say, "Well it's convenient." *Yes, and do you need it? Are you any more satisfied by being able to decide what you want and order it immediately?*

Kozmo.com are a company whose basic business premise is that when people decide they want something, they want their need gratified there and then. So their unique selling point is that they will deliver to you within one hour. Their range of goods started with videos, ice cream and popcorn; it is now a fuller grocery service. Instant gratification is certainly a feature of the E world. *Why is it so important, and what happens if you don't get it?* Just as you are who you are, you are also who you are in the way you connect to others. You cannot connect to anyone who is not also connecting with you. If you wish to connect, you have to consider the other person's frame of reference. That is hard if you are looking to them for instant gratification, whether in the form of information, money or affection.

Any drug addict will tell you that the wonder of the rush is always followed by the down of where the next one is coming from. *If your life focuses on NOW, there is no perspective, nothing more than what comes next.*

"ONE CANNOT BE HUMAN BY ONESELF.
THERE IS NO SELFHOOD
WHERE THERE IS NO COMMUNITY."

[JAMES CARSE]

Ok, of course there are those who take themselves out of society, but we are looking at people who want something from the larger community, whether it is money, fame or food etc. It is, however, WE who create the connection flow. It is not incidents or technology. It is us. So no discussion of the effect of E business, the Internet or the wired world can occur without acknowledging that currently people make up this wired community, and as such are subject to the same slings and arrows that any relationship would have. *So where does technology have its biggest impact?* Mind you, being part of what many describe as a "community" online means you are part of a giant global marketing experiment.

"WE'VE BUILT MASSIVE WEB SITES WITH MILLIONS OF RELATIONSHIPS TO CONSUMERS. NOW, WE'RE FINDING WAYS TO MAKE THOSE RELATIONSHIPS PROFITABLE."
[BO PEABODY, CEO OF TRIPOD, A COMMUNITY OWNED BY LYCOS]

I wonder what he means by relationships? How do you feel being used so publicly for profit? Is it any different from any other sales exploitation, apart from scale?

Marketers are swimming in data on people who sign up to sites or chat rooms. They can visit bulletin boards, chat rooms, personal home pages, photo galleries and with smart software tools can use these snippets for tips on consumer trends. Sometimes site owners do it for them. In this way, Tripod has managed to sort over 85% of its Web pages into categories. There have already been scandals where the Federal Trade Commission in the US accused site owners of selling members' personal information to outside markets. The accused, GeoCities, did deny the charges, but agreed to bolster privacy agreements. Sometimes, the consumer reacts more directly. One analyst wrote that if you put a Coca-Cola advert into a chat room, participants quickly start to "flame" Coke.

Of course, E commerce companies call this part of the relationship-building process. I am not aware of many long-term relationships that are built by one of the parties collecting data on the other without them knowing...

Given the anonymous nature of the Web, I also wonder how accurate the data is on individuals, particularly in terms of their likes and dislikes. Certainly, in the case of E commerce, the rewards for the "relationship" are all material, and therefore the relationship stays as a commercial transactional one, at a surface level.

Mary Modahl, in her book *Now or Never*, describes how Forrester Research have coined a term for the approach they use for studying people's attitudes about technology to determine who uses the Net; they call it technographics. They suggest that consumers have either positive or negative attitudes towards technology, and that they fall into one of three categories: "early adopters", "mainstream" and "laggards". Within the segments are groups whose differing needs drive how they will or won't use technology. For example, in the early adopter segment are "fast forwards", who use technology to advance their careers; "new age nurturers", who are more family-oriented; and "mouse potatoes", who use technology for entertainment. Some of the first, and most bizarre, TV commercials were from online music stores, who were obviously looking to chase the "mouse potatoes", who want to be entertained, watch a lot of TV and spend even more time online. E music makes money by relying on the Internet to slash marketing, manufacturing and distribution costs. *Who needs ads, when searches for "MP3", the leading format for music downloads, now outnumber all other search items, even the word "sex"?* So much for the Internet being about pornography...

By the time you read this book, who knows what the numbers will look like? Who really knows whether they are correct? Still, it's nice to know that even in the E world, we still need to be categorized.....

"COMPUTERS ARE WORTHLESS,

When John Naisbitt, the author of the bestseller *Megatrends*, was asked in 1999 about why he did not use the Internet for collection of data for his new book, he replied, "No, we didn't look at the Internet. The Internet is really too primitive and random." Explaining why, he commented: "Why would we want to spend more time staring at a screen?" It is very hard to describe and comment on something you don't know or haven't experienced with any validity. Many people dismiss different parts of the E world, because they have no significance in their lives, or they don't want them to, or they don't understand them. They are there. *What relationship do you want to have to this world?*

THEY ONLY GIVE YOU ANSWERS."

[PABLO PICASSO]

"IF THERE IS SOMETHING DISTURBING ABOUT FINDING COMMUNITY THROUGH A COMPUTER SCREEN, WE SHOULD ALSO CONSIDER WHETHER IT IS DISTURBING FOR MILLIONS OF PEOPLE TO DRIVE FOR HOURS IN THEIR SINGLE PASSENGER, INTERNAL COMBUSTION ENGINES TO CITIES OF INHUMAN SCALE, WHERE THEY SPEND THEIR DAYS IN FRONT OF SCREENS IN CUBICLES WITHIN SKYSCRAPERS FULL OF PEOPLE WHO DO NOT KNOW EACH OTHER. THE RUBBER TYRE AND THE LIFT BOTH PLAYED THEIR PART IN THE CONSTRUCTION OF A TECHNOLOGY-CENTRIC COMMUNITY."

[HOWARD RHEINGOLD]

Travelling long distances to work, working long hours, feeling pushed to the limit, all have an enormous impact on the way we relate to each other.

Steve is a very bright financial marketing analyst. He started life in a large Silicon Valley corporation, which was not renowned for its tender mercies. That toughened him up, but at least in the tightness of the corporation he had a large family set-up, with rules, norms and values that were very apparent, and everyone stuck to them, or left the organization (voluntarily or otherwise). You worked unbelievably long hours, you always over-achieved, you always competed with your colleagues, and you were very protective of the company and those who worked in it to the outside world. He could have been working for any large corporation. Maybe the speed was ramped up a little because of the speed of the industry, so it just emphasized something that was already present.

He was headhunted out for large sums of money and a senior vice-president title and joined a start-up venture capital organization. He suddenly found himself without the safety net and huge arms of the corporation. Devoid of the sibling 'relationships' and the competition, he was left competing with himself, and set himself an incredibly punishing schedule that had him flying to Europe once a week for two days. This left him very work- focused, and even when he was at home he was still competing with himself by training for marathon running. He maintained his connections with his out-of-work friends, many of whom had either worked for or still worked for his former employer. His attitude to them was "I am at home; why won't you fit into my schedule?" He was lucky that his charm and long standing with his friends kept a circle going that was totally Steve-focused. He made no new friends, in a social sense, and the few romantic relationships he embarked on were very intense to begin with and then fizzled out, as they could not compete with either Steve or his schedule. He is always "just about to take a holiday".

You all know a Steve. You may be a Steve. Steve is confronted with choice: he is fortunate to be healthy, smart and attractive. He does not know what he wants. The E world has brought him wealth and a seemingly successful career. He does not know what success needs to be for him. In the pace and trappings of the E universe, he is left with just that: pace and trappings. He feels empty but doesn't know how or what would fill him up........

"IT IS DIFFICULT

TO GET THE NEWS FROM POEMS.

YET MEN DIE MISERABLY EVERY DAY

FOR LACK

OF WHAT IS FOUND THERE."

[DAVID WHYTE]

So what is it that makes the difference in the E world? Is there such a big difference? Have you just transferred the same old same old to a faster environment?

"WE SHALL NOT CEASE FROM EXPLORATION
AND THE END OF ALL OUR EXPLORING
WILL BE TO ARRIVE WHERE WE STARTED
AND KNOW THE PLACE FOR THE FIRST TIME."
[T.S. ELIOT]

Where do you start in this book? Normally when people read books, they are forced down a linear, time-fixed route; alone. Every person's route through this book will be unique, and they will have the opportunity to connect to others and share their journey, at the same time as they are updating their knowledge.... a never ending story..... There are way more questions, because it's not only difficult but also misleading to provide answers; this is a journey which revolves around human beings, so there are no answers.

Everyone's need is different. Everyone has a different expectation from their workplace and their world. The way we connect is a crucial part of this.

TRANSCRIPT OF AN ACTUAL RADIO CONVERSATION BETWEEN A US NAVY SHIP AND CANADIAN AUTHORITIES OFF THE COAST OF NEWFOUNDLAND:

[US SHIP] PLEASE DIVERT YOUR COURSE 0.5 DEGREES TO THE SOUTH TO AVOID A COLLISION.
[CANADIAN] RECOMMEND YOU DIVERT YOUR COURSE 15 DEGREES TO THE SOUTH TO AVOID COLLISION.
[US SHIP] THIS IS THE CAPTAIN OF A US NAVY SHIP.
I SAY AGAIN DIVERT YOUR COURSE.
[CANADIAN] NO I SAY AGAIN, DIVERT YOUR COURSE.

[US SHIP] THIS IS THE AIRCRAFT CARRIER USS MISSOURI. WE ARE A LARGE WARSHIP OF THE US NAVY. DIVERT YOUR COURSE NOW.
[CANADIAN] THIS IS A LIGHTHOUSE. YOUR CALL.

[FROM *ISLAND TIMES*]

There is no right or wrong way to relate and connect; only the most appropriate one for the situation. To understand and analyze what this appropriate behaviour is, you need to be tuned in to both self and others. The people who have the most effective relationships are great listeners and observers. They know when to speak and when to make their move. They know when to project their view and when to respond in the other person's framework. This doesn't happen without a great deal of self-awareness; that enables you to respond fast, but without projection.

Awareness is not something you can pick up from Awareness.com, although many people will tell you of sites that will provide... It only happens by opening your mind to self and others. It's not about the right answers; it's about the right questions... *What are the right questions for you? Do you know what are the most important things in your life? Do you treat them as such? Do you know how technology has impacted on your life (for better and worse)?*

"DOWN WITH ALL KINGS BUT KING LUDD."
[BYRON]

One of the interesting features of this technological "revolution" is that most people accept it. There are few vocal Luddites, and no organized counter-revolution. *Why should this be?* People talk and write about individual freedom in the virtual world, and in the same breath say we all have to get on the bus; that would certainly suggest a lack of choice... *What does it mean to get on the bus, and what will it mean if we don't?* The more possibilities you provide, the more you have to keep up; just like the automotive revolution, more cars means more roads, but not necessarily easier travel as they are so crowded. To shift a paradigm would be to destroy what they are....... *TV brings in uninvited guests to the home – what does technology bring in?* Get the most out of life – put the most in....

What would the most look like? Would you know it if you were experiencing it? How would you know what to look for? What do you want the most? Do relationships have an intrinsic value in themselves or do they need to have focus and outcome?

Work relationships have a built-in basic contract: do the work you have agreed to do and you get paid. How you achieve that is sometimes up for negotiation. The same is true of personal relationships, except the payment is usually recognition, acceptance and love.

"YOU HAVE NO FEELINGS AT ALL."
"YES I DO; I HAVE MY FEELINGS, AND THEY ARE NOT YOURS."
"WHAT KIND OF RELATIONSHIP IS THIS?"
"ADEQUATE."

[OVERHEARD CONVERSATION]

Is achievement the only measure of success? So with all these questions about relating to others in the E world, what actually is a relationship? In one thesaurus, the following words get pulled up: association, affiliation, relevance, connection, conjunction, dependence, coherence, affinity, kinship, interdependence, attraction, bond, attachment.

What creates these things in a wired world? Is it any different to the one we have known hitherto? Are these the things we will seek in the future? How does technology impact on them?

What pulls together Time, Space, Depth and Pace?

The distinction we make between self and others becomes very blurred once we realize how interconnected people, events and thought are. We all have a sense of self, but it exists in connection with the rest of the world. The Space we live in, the Pace at which we do things, how we choose to spend our Time, the Depth of relationships we have, want or need. Our identity is built on various premises of the ways in which we connect to the world.

We mark ourselves by our relationship with our context, and vice versa. Some of the pressure that the E world presents is a feeling of being dragged along by our context. Yet it is we who build and shape the context. *Where do you begin on this Möbius strip of reality?*

"IF THE SELF HAD INTRINSIC IDENTITY,

IT WOULD BE POSSIBLE TO SPEAK IN TERMS OF SELF-INTEREST IN ISOLATION FROM THAT OF OTHERS. BUT BECAUSE THIS IS NOT SO, BECAUSE SELF AND OTHERS CAN ONLY BE UNDERSTOOD IN TERMS OF RELATIONSHIP, WE SEE THAT SELF-INTEREST AND OTHERS' INTERESTS ARE CLOSELY INTERRELATED INDEED, WITHIN THIS PICTURE OF DEPENDENTLY ORIGINATED REALITY, WE SEE THAT THERE IS NO SELF-INTEREST COMPLETELY UNRELATED TO OTHERS' INTERESTS. DUE TO THE FUNDAMENTAL INTERCONNECTEDNESS THAT LIES AT THE HEART OF REALITY, YOUR INTEREST IS ALSO MY INTEREST. FROM THIS, IT BECOMES CLEAR THAT 'MY ' INTEREST AND 'YOUR' INTEREST ARE FUNDAMENTALLY CONNECTED. IN A DEEP SENSE, THEY CONVERGE."

[THE DALAI LAMA]

Individuals and their choices: We can choose when, where and how. Ability to choose reduces stress; too much choice creates stress. *What pulls and pushes us in different directions? Is that choice?* Choice of what we do, when we do it, how we do it and who we do it with. *What drives the choice? What does it take to make it? What stops you making it? What effect does new technology have on choice?*

So what has been the attraction of the Web? Is it the technology? Is it the graphics? Is it something far more basic? For the vast majority of users it is unlikely to be the technology *per se*, or the graphics *per se*. It is far more likely to be the spirit of connection.

Spiriting the connection and connecting the spirit... The Internet and its progeny have connected people to each other and provided a way in which people could find and use their own voices. It does not do it for them. *The Cluetrain Manifesto* describes it as: *"To all its inhabitants, it is primarily a place in which all are audience to each other. The entertainment is not packaged, it is intrinsic."* People find themselves at liberty to learn, laugh and compare. Because of the technical efficiency of the Internet, organizations use it to become more productive, faster. They need the intellectual capital that has become the key to being successful in the "Knowledge Economy". (They seem to have missed the point that the knowledge is actually created by people, who are therefore the most valuable asset...but of this more later.) *What does this mean for individuals and organizations?*

The Web, by its nature, is non-bureaucratic. It encourages speculation, debate and individuality. People who take to the Web are more comfortable with risk than rules. Many companies are frightened by these changes, seeing them as a loss of control. It is. Well, for the organizations, that is. Some individuals see it as a loss of control. Seeing as how it's individuals that make up organizations......

How should trade be conducted? How can you manage intellectual property (if you so desire)? How should online communities define their boundaries? How can political discussions take place?

It is becoming harder to separate workplace and homeplace, as the technology often exists in both places. It is becoming harder to distinguish between work time and free time, and where we "consume" and where we "produce". Ambiguous and competing zones have already started to emerge. For example, people are online at work and go home and go online. Their intent may be different, but they are still operating in the same ether space. You might argue that their intent is the same. They want to acquire knowledge, possessions or friendship.

The convergence of homeplace and workplace promises a world in which commerce becomes an integrated part of the lives of individuals and communities. This blurring confuses where we stand as individuals.

This is a book about the way people behave with each other: about the spirit in which people and businesses are working and its implications. *What does doing business in this way mean for relationships, both personal and professional? How does it change the way we look at, talk to and respond to each other? Does it matter any more? Why is it of interest? Do we need relationships any more? If so, what kind? If not, what does that mean for the type of life we lead?*

> "THE FUTURE BUSINESS OF BUSINESSES THAT HAVE A FUTURE WILL BE ABOUT SUBTLE DIFFERENCES, NOT WHOLESALE CONFORMITY; ABOUT DIVERSITY, NOT HOMOGENEITY; ABOUT BREAKING RULES, NOT ENFORCING THEM; ABOUT PUSHING THE ENVELOPE, NOT PUNCHING THE CLOCK; ABOUT INVITATION, NOT PROTECTION; ABOUT DOING IT FIRST, NOT DOING IT 'RIGHT'; ABOUT MAKING IT BETTER, NOT MAKING IT PERFECT; ABOUT TELLING THE TRUTH, NOT SPINNING BIGGER LIES; ABOUT TURNING PEOPLE ON, NOT 'PACKAGING' THEM; AND PERHAPS ABOVE ALL, ABOUT BUILDING CONVIVIAL COMMUNITIES AND KNOWLEDGE ECOLOGIES ONLINE, NOT LEVERAGING DEMOGRAPHIC SECTORS THERE."
>
> [THE *CLUETRAIN MANIFESTO*]

Brave words, from brave people; totally dependent on the desire of people to make it happen. If large corporations and governments are not responsible for you, then only you are.... *do you want to be? What will happen to those who don't want the responsibility or know how to take it? So how can organizations manage this encouragement of liberty? How can individuals manage this encouragement of liberty? Where will it take us? Where will we take it? Getting beyond the hype....what is really going on out there? Does anyone know? Is anyone stopping for long enough to observe? What would they see?* Time is tight but the new economy is quick...

These questions, and many more, will be answered on a website near you.....

Seriously, the book is about providing insight into how people are relating to one another in this wired world, and what the impact of that is, and might be, now and in the future. It asks way more questions than you might be comfortable with, but in the E world, no one wants to make the decision for you, or so it seems; at least they want you to think that you are the one making the decision.

What are the key questions for you? How will you go about answering and/or accepting them?

When Po Bronson describes Silicon Valley, he could be describing the whole E world...It's "about the opportunity to become a mover, not about being one".

It is that opportunity which defines the E world; a world of possibility, with no guarantees. Building and developing relationships around possibility leaves people more guarded. Intention is hidden, and possibly based on success: not much chance of unconditional regard there...

There is no 'so what', or end to this book. There are no how to's. Living in the E world means understanding where you are in relation to the opportunities it can bring and, like every double-edged sword, the destructiveness it can wreak.

Ask yourself the questions; stop blaming "it". Live there and enjoy it for what it is, not for your fantasy.

> "THE ONLY ZEN YOU FIND AT THE TOP OF THE MOUNTAIN
> IS THE ZEN YOU TOOK UP THERE."
> **[ROBERT PIRSIG]**

In *Politics Without a Past*, Shari Cohen examines what happens to democracies whose history was swept away by the onset of communism; she explores the impact of building a country without its historical social glue. In many ways the impact of technology on our lives is similar. There are no historical parallels that match the effect of technology on our lives, and in many ways the early adopters are inventing their past, by focusing on the future. We don't have any history or "glue" to frame our decisions. This often results in what appear to be risky decisions based on little data...maybe there is none. There are no precedents. Maybe we have to get past the idea of being judged against something, as there is no something there. There is only us, and the world current and future.......

"AS THEY
REACHED
THE MOUNTAINSIDE,
A WONDROUS
PORTAL
OPENED WIDE...."

[*SWEET HEREAFTER*]

[DEPTH]

AND RELATIONSHIPS

"WELL WHAT IS ANYTHING FOR?
WHAT IS WRITING FOR?
WHAT IS THEATRE FOR?
WHAT IS MUSIC FOR?

IT IS TO ENABLE YOU TO HAVE A DEEPER SENSE OF WHO YOU ARE, AND THE PLACE YOU LIVE IN AND THE PEOPLE AROUND YOU, AND HAVE A SENSE OF THEM AND SOLIDARITY WITH THEM AND UNDERSTANDING AND WARMTH. BECAUSE THOSE ARE THE ONLY THINGS WE'VE GOT."

[KEN LOACH]

Given the blurring of home and workplace, and how the E world exists in both places, it is worth exploring how technology and the E world have affected the depth and kind of relationships we seek and have, both in and out of the workplace. After all, our desires are the same, but the manifestations are different. Sometimes, the pace of the workplace creates the different relationship need outside, or changes the nature of those relationships, whether it is having to find a partner online, because that is where you spend your time, or not being able to shop or be with your family.

So much juggling to be done. So much deciding about what is and isn't important. So many choices. So many people and things to consider. *How do you decide what's important?*

If Internet access and the E world in general have moved us from finite numbers of relationships to infinite, you increase the number of opportunities to connect. *Is it possible to maintain an infinite number of relationships? At what level do you want those relationships? How do you decide the depth of a relationship?* For many people, the Internet has changed their means or given them a new means of making (or breaking) relationships and communication. *You are besieged on all sides by opportunities to connect; how do you get and keep the spirit of connection?*

"THERE'S MORE BANDWIDTH WALKING DOWN 5TH AVENUE
THAN YOU'LL EVER GET ON YOUR COMPUTER."
[STEVE WEBER]

What does living in an E world do to the level of relationships you have and seek? Do you seek anything different? Do you do it in a different way?

The Internet is potentially your sublimest fantasy... success, your wildest dreams, everything you ever wanted, available now, through your fingers on the keyboard.... That is a pretty seductive premise; only a miserable person would not want it to be true. *Is it true? And if your fantasy is available, what happens then?*

FANTASY ......DREAMING YOUR DREAMS: FANTASY OF COMMUNITY
FANTASY OF LOVE
FANTASY OF PROFIT

Anthony Storr suggests that an inner world of fantasy must be regarded as part of an individual's biological inheritance. When an individual's subjective reality becomes completely divorced from the external reality, we call them mad. On the other hand, if we suppress the inner world too much we become totally compliant with external reality; we regard the external world as something to which we must adapt, so our individuality disappears and life becomes meaningless.

The E world seems to make all fantasies more attainable, without you taking the time to see if they are actually what you want... This leads back to the spirit of connection. There is no real difference between this seductive promise and the romantic ideal that you get fed from movies, books and advertising. Our expectation that satisfying intimate relationships should ideally provide happiness – and if they do not, there must be something wrong with the relationships – is as exaggerated as is the sales Internet fantasy, or the vast riches dream of the over-committed high achievers. In all cases, it damages the precious relationships we do have, whether work-based or personal, by putting pressure on them as the make or break of our lives.

LEVELS OF SHALLOWNESS

Success, friendship and love are important parts of our lives. We do change and develop as our lives continue. This uncertainty is inherent in any relationship. No one element of this triangle is usually enough. It is the balance of the triangle, and that doesn't necessarily mean it is an equilateral triangle. Its shape should represent our needs, and what is important at that point. The E world seems to throw us out of kilter, and make us not pay attention or even know what is really important. So nothing has any depth, and you end up feeling and being shallow.

"YOUR SUBCONSCIOUS IS SO CLOSE TO THE SURFACE
THAT I CAN SEE ITS PERISCOPE."

[SPALDING GRAY]

"HE'S BRIGHT ENOUGH TO KNOW HIS LIMITATIONS,
BUT NOT GIFTED ENOUGH TO OVERCOME THEM."

[LAURA GUYER MILLER]

Email is most people's introduction to the Internet, and usually remains a constant, so deserves pride of place in any exploration of relationships in the E world. It also allows you to feel "wanted" ("you've got mail") very quickly and stops a lot of people feeling lonely; *but what does it give them? Does it give them a relationship, or the illusion of one? Does it matter?* Well only if it is being used to hide from or diminish a real-world relationship... it's like having an affair in the office without having the affair...no blue dresses online.... *So how about the ultimate relationship fantasy on the Internet: romance?*

One piece of helpful equipment might be this product from a company called Skim.com, based in Zurich. Let's say you are sitting on a crowded Tube train and want to say hi to a cute stranger. *Do you (a) fight the crowd to tap him on the shoulder; (b) shout across the train car; or (c) send him an email?* If he is wearing something from Net fashion start-up Skim.com, the answer could be (c). It has created a range of bags with identification numbers to create what it hopes will be the next-generation answer to personal ads. You buy a Skim.com item with a unique six-digit number on it. Activate the number at the website and it becomes your email address. Then all you have to do is hit the streets, and hope secret admirers contact you, while your personal info remains anonymous. Of course wearing this kind of item could signal to the world that you are incapable of meeting people in a normal way. The makers even have a reason for wearing a number, which we often associate with prisoners or robots. They feel it takes courage to be on the leading edge, and that a number will therefore make the product more desirable. Hmmmm...

So many stories and at least one big-time movie about love on the Net... *does it, can it, happen? How does the Internet affect the most intimate of relationships?*

"VIRTUAL COMMUNICATION

OF INTIMACY."

CREATES AN ILLUSION

[K.T. MILLER]

VIRTUAL INTIMACY

Because of the intensity with which people pursue a relationship in an Ethernet vacuum, they can only end up with fantasy. People disclose a great deal to each other, but it can only be at a cerebral level, even if the data is about emotions. So the individuals believe that they are on a much deeper level than they actually are. Many "relationships" which begin on email, and seem very promising, need real time before people know whether this "close" relationship on the Net will translate to the real world. People may communicate perfectly, feel as though they have a rapport with someone, even feel understood, but humans need face-to-face interaction to determine whether the person is truly connected. So much of our communication takes place on a subliminal level, which doesn't happen in an online transaction, that the ensuing "relationship" is devoid of a key factor.

Steve and Angela met online, met up fairly soon after their online meeting, and then pursued a conventional relationship with all its ups and downs, and are now very happily married with a child.

Susie and David met online, and became totally besotted with each other. They seemed to think the same way, want the same things and laugh at the same things. They eventually met, and by this time really wanted the relationship to work. They both felt they had found a soulmate online. To their relief, everything seemed ok, and so they continued to plan as any couple might, for the future. They shared the fantasy that if you fall in love, everything will fall into place. It almost seemed that once they had "secured" that fantasy, i.e. met each other, the rest would work itself out. At this point, their guard went down and some of the cracks started to appear. The jury is still out....

Fran and Jeff met through a business correspondence online. They enjoyed each other's humour and attitude to people and life, and soon their communication was solely about each other, not work. This happened over a period of weeks and very soon they were exchanging emails daily, and really becoming addicted to the receipt of emails. There was plenty of emotion within the minds of the two individuals, and indeed in their emails, but was it what one would call a relationship? Of course it was: they were connecting with each other, for sure, and enjoying the connection. But whether it was a small part of their being, just an online part of them, or was true to their whole selves was unclear to both of them. They even discussed it online, and after a frantic couple of days which involved an exchange of almost 40 emails, they both felt emotionally exhausted, and decided to resort to a more mundane form of communication, which would at least add one more sense to their knowledge of each other. They spoke for a couple of hours on the phone, and this seemed to calm down the freneticism that the exchange of emails had generated. They have since agreed to meet.........The movie is not over yet... So they got together through a workplace connection and technology. *How will real time and visuals affect their "relationship"? Does being aware of its limitations stop the fantasy? Is it ok just to enjoy the fantasy?*

Well this could happen in any relationship, on or offline, in or out of work; two people wanting a fantasy, not a reality, not asking enough questions... it seems that what relationships on the Net do is make all the loopholes a little larger. Digital dating has the same hazards as analogue dating – it's just that there are many more places to hide. Interestingly, many people either know or know of someone who has had some kind of romantic relationship via the Internet. (While this book was being edited, this section received the most emotive responses from everyone who read it. It seems that identification with and a need for personal relationships are still a huge part of our lives in the E world.)

Email can start a conversation, but you need the phone call or presence to provoke dialogue and thought. It is this provocation that sometimes seems absent in email communication; maybe not absent, so much as one-dimensional. You can misread cues or perceived cues. There is no way of checking out without asking, and that may not get a validation that feels strong enough for you to proceed or let go... The effect someone's voice can have on a communication is very dramatic. We pick up more from voice tone than we do from dress. Dress is more to do with surface bias. Tone of voice hits something deeper in the mind. Put the people in the room together and the intensity is dramatically heightened.

"IT IS NOT EASY TO KNOW WHAT YOU LIKE.

MOST PEOPLE FOOL THEMSELVES THEIR ENTIRE LIVES ABOUT THIS.
SELF-ACQUAINTANCE IS A RARE CONDITION."

[ROBERT HENRI]

E MYTH OR E MAIL

So this isn't about email good or bad. It's about what it is useful for. As with many things we as humans have explored and uncovered, we want to believe that there is something, just the one thing, out there that, if we had it, would resolve everything. All our problems would be over. Look at our mythology: the Holy Grail, the Ark of the Covenant, the Messiah and the Second Coming. Ok, these are all religious panaceas, but most major scientific breakthroughs are hailed in a similar way, for good and evil. The Internet has been given the status of both Saviour and Destructor, which tends to be how we see our religious icons too. *Logically speaking, how could any one thing be the answer to everything?* There is no perfect solution (although mathematicians and physicists might argue that one). There is no perfect relationship; in fact it is the idiosyncrasies of the relationship which make it special. We seek "perfect" and "right", but are not sure we know what that would look like if we found it. *What would the questioning, exploring, learning human soul do if it did find an answer to everything? I guess it's like getting what you always wanted, and then looking around and saying "Is that all there is?" What comes next?* As a species, we are constantly seeking improvement and enlightenment in many different ways. *Why should we expect The answer from any one person or thing?*

Do you know someone better after three weeks of intense emailing or two dates? When people answer personal ads, they often disclose more about themselves in their first telephone call than they might do if they met someone at a party. As with email, it is almost as if you give out more data as you have no other senses to make assessments with. It still doesn't mean you know anyone....you only learn about someone by being with them.

One of the interesting things about engaging others is that when we engage out of choice, we usually have more fun and are more playful. This tends to be because we have no expectation in advance of where the relationship may lead. In fact, there is no expected outcome apart from agreeing to be a party to it. In this level of relationship, everything matters, because nothing is of more or less importance. If people take up a chat room or email relationship from this vantage point, it can be great fun. It is when the expected outcome changes to something more serious that disappointment may appear. Becoming serious usually means that you have a specified outcome in mind, and therefore are at risk of it not happening....... Without feeling and hope, all the data and success in the world leave a being feeling empty, even Vulcans. *So what about rejection?*

"IF I WASN'T SCARED, THEN IT WOULDN'T BE AN EXPERIENCE AND I WOULDN'T GROW."
[LAUREN PHILLIPS]

"GET USED TO DISAPPOINTMENT."
[THE PRINCESS BRIDE]

Email, because of its lack of face-to-face, of course can have some positive impact in that it can allow people for whom face-to-face contact is very threatening to communicate without the fear of being present. Of course, translated, this means that they are not really facing up to whatever it is they are frightened of, and indeed can even retreat better because they can say "but I told you on email...."

Peter forgot his sister's birthday, which was a cardinal sin in their family. He felt bad, but instead of phoning up his sister and telling her exactly that, he sent her an email entitled "I am such an idiot". He never actually spoke to her about it, and on the surface, it looked like he was confessing. I guess it's like a child (or grown-up) feeling that as soon as you have said "I'm sorry" it's all over. (Some religions do believe this to be true.) This isn't about major remorse for forgetting a birthday; it's about respecting what is important to another person, and acknowledging your part in that. If you are now headed for the "yeah well, that's nice but I haven't got time for all that" place, it doesn't make sense. To actually be clear and face things as they happen stops a long drawn out process, conscious and otherwise. (Yes, she is still smarting that he didn't care enough to make the phone call...)

" 'YOU NEVER KNOW
WHO ANYBODY IS.'
'WHO IS WHAT THEY SEEM?
WHO IN THE WORLD
IS WHAT THEY SEEM?' "

[DAVID MAMET, *THE SPANISH PRISONER*]

Everyone has many email horror and joy stories: the grandparents who found an inexpensive way to maintain regular contact with their dispersed family, including seeing pictures, the member of the office team who felt that the email they were sent was much too harsh about their behaviour, the email that got accidentally copied to the individual it was being derogatory about, the student who kept track of her travelling companions through email.

One senior manager described the positive aspects of email in this way: "In our company, the way one manager, for example, uses email to communicate directly with the sales reps, to involve them and to get them on side, could never have been achieved with the memo or telephone. What's more, I think email is a great force for democratizing the enterprise. Not just because it makes it easy to send messages directly to people and bypass the hierarchy, but because the language we use is much more conversational, much less formal. Formality and hierarchy in business are huge barriers to (real) relationships. Email in particular helps undermine both.

The fact that it's the perfect medium for group communications also makes it the perfect medium for organizing social affairs. So we use it as much to arrange a drink after work as we do for official business, blurring once more the divide between work and play, colleagues and friends. What belongs to the role and what belongs to me inevitably start to converge."

Some people say the telephone is impersonal, others feel it is too personal. Some people actually find email less impersonal than the telephone. When questioned further, they usually say that they feel that it leaves the writer the ability to do it at their own time and pace, without interruption. I wonder if that suggests that they feel exposed on the telephone. On email you are alone with your thoughts and feelings; you choose what you want to share, are not under pressure to respond immediately, and are safe from the unwanted intrusion of another human being.

ETHERCLOAKS OF ANONYMITY

Deborah Tannen, author of *The Argument Culture*, suggests that along with the networks of loving human connection, the Internet also creates hostile and distressing communication. Some of this is to do with the anonymity of email, which again serves as both a positive and a negative. There are many stories of chat room "stalking"; that is, people continuing to send a person unwanted email from a chat room connection. It is easier to feel and express hostility for someone who you don't know personally, not unlike the rage some drivers feel towards an anonymous car that has cut them up in traffic. If you give the finger to someone in a car, and you realize that you know the person, the rush of shame you experience is evidence that anonymity was essential for both your expression and experience of rage.

"YOU CAN FIND YOURSELF LOOKING AT THINGS
THAT SEEM TO BE MERE APPEARANCES, EXPRESSIONS OF NOTHING,
FACES WITH NOTHING BEHIND THEM."

[EUGÈNE IONESCO]

Technology has the ability to pull people together, but the more people are deprived of contact, the harder it can become to resolve difficulty. Everything is fine while everything is fine, but at the first sign of conflict, a lack of physical presence is likely to increase antagonism, not decrease it. It is much easier to "demonize" an individual when you haven't met them. You have no connection and therefore no responsibility to them. In a larger picture it is that distance which keeps people in pain and unable to resolve major conflicts, such as bringing Palestinians and Israelis together. In the workplace, using email to "resolve" conflicts inevitably escalates them as the potential for misunderstanding and assumption grows.

The more our technology increases our ability to do things individually, the more we get pulled apart from our social encounters...even on the most trivial scale. I watched a man in the supermarket on his portable phone talking to someone as he described everything on the deli counter. *Why could they not have the conversation together?* Even more extreme, I was standing in a queue in a French bakery, again watching a man talk to someone about which kind of loaf they wanted. As we both walked out of the shop, and he walked to his car, I realized the person he was talking to was sitting outside in the car..... It can also make us think that we are more powerful than we are: the technology does not change Us. It can change our ability to do things.

In *Why Things Bite Back*, Edward Tenner observes that technology aggravates aggressive driving: with antilock brakes and improved steering, many drivers become overconfident in their ability to drive safely.

One organization used email to signal a change in management style after a CEO change. It looked as though this was a more modern, open style of communication. Unfortunately the initial behaviour was not backed up with any supporting behaviours. In fact, the communications on email began to look suspiciously like the old communications, except they weren't on paper. *Won't get fooled again, huh?*

"NEVER HAVE SO MANY
HAD SO MUCH POWER
TO VIOLATE
THEIR OWN PRIVACY!"

[ANON.]

TELL IT LIKE IT REALLY REALLY IS

Most companies, if they get down to examining where their breakdowns in communication are (if they get that far) find that the worst ones are the ones that were fully online or in memos, or at least started there. Some people find that the forced pace of E business makes you more honest and blunt in business communication. If you are balancing so many projects, all with potentially competing priorities and timelines, then an ability to be to the point is very valuable. The issue is not being honest, it's the way in which it is done. It is a skill to be blunt concisely, particularly online. There are many books that tell you the protocols for doing this, but there are two fundamental principles that would make a huge difference:

1. KNOW EXACTLY WHAT YOU WANT THE OTHER PERSON TO DO AS A RESULT OF SENDING YOUR MESSAGE. OFTEN WE SEND OFF THE MESSAGE SAYING WHAT WE WANT RATHER THAN WHAT WE WANT THE PERSON TO DO.

2. THINK THROUGH WHAT THEIR RESPONSES MIGHT BE, AND USE APPROPRIATE LANGUAGE.

Voicemail is similar, but leaving a voice message connects you to the message in a way that an email doesn't. Again, in the heat of anger, it is sometimes both easy and tempting to call someone and tell them what you think. Sometimes people feel better saying that to a machine, and in fact tone it down when they actually have contact with the other person. Sometimes the lengthy process of "snailmail" allows you to vent, but it takes longer to send it, and by that time, you may feel differently, and/or wish to change your message. That's hard to do when you have fired off an email or left an angry voicemail message. There is no way to take back what you said, or correct misinterpretations. There is also no response to give perspective. It also depends on what your intent was in sending the message. Often, when we are enraged, all we want to do is punish the person who has caused us pain. We sometimes shroud that in "I need to tell them how I feel" but what is usually said is a blame statement, not a statement of feelings. A response can help the communication. It is very easy when hunched over a computer screen to let your anger flow out. Try it, if you haven't already. Again it is the anonymity that increases the hostility.

Wendy and Martin were trying hard to sort out a complex work relationship. One day, angry that Wendy had not arrived at the conclusion he wished her to have done, Martin fired off a very angry missive. Whilst he described it as just wanting to tell things how they were, it was clear that he really wanted to punish Wendy for not being strong enough. It took 24 hours and a discussion with a friend to appreciate that the effect the email was likely to have might be counter-productive to the long-term result he wanted. He would never have said those things to her face or even voice. He had had the opportunity that same day but hadn't taken it. Now she was travelling and was difficult to reach, and he wanted to reverse what he had said with the same passion as he had sent the first message. He ended up sending her a second email, which was much more responsive to her position. Unfortunately, she read the first one first, and it totally blew the effect of the second. She didn't read it. The damage was done. She was already hurt, and felt Martin did not understand. She used her physical absence to remain absent from their discussions, and blamed his lack of understanding. It may well have been a way of her avoiding some of the difficulties she had, but it was an option that presented itself and she took it. Again, the anonymity had allowed a rage to be expressed in a way that would not have happened face to face. It is easy to forget that behind every computer screen (well most) lies a person.

Deborah Tannen, in her book *The Argument Culture*, observes that "The rising level of public aggression in our society seems directly related to the increasing isolation in our lives, which is helped along by advances in technology. This isolation – and the technology that enhances it – is an ingredient in the argument culture. We seem to be better at developing technological means of communication than at finding ways to temper the hostility that sometimes accompanies them. We have to work harder at finding those ways. That is the challenge we now face."

"... AND TO THE GOOD WHO KNOW HOW WIDE
THE GULF, HOW DEEP
BETWEEN IDEAL AND REAL, WHO BEING
GOOD HAVE FELT
THE FINAL TEMPTATION TO WITHDRAW, SIT
DOWN AND WEEP,

WE PRAY THE POWER TO TAKE UPON
THEMSELVES THE GUILT
OF HUMAN ACTION, THOUGH STILL
AS READY TO CONFESS
THE IMPERFECTION OF WHAT CAN
AND MUST BE BUILT,
THE WISH AND POWER TO ACT, FORGIVE,
AND BLESS."

[W.H. AUDEN AND LOUIS MACNEICE, LAST WILL AND TESTAMENT]

Bang and Olufsen have an answerphone which allows the owner to refuse calls from certain telephone numbers. This is an extension of caller ID, which allows you to identify who is calling you. *What makes you take up these expensive options? Is it the fear of who might be calling you, or a need to control your environment, so that only people you choose can enter? "It's my time, and I choose"?*

Again, this is not about right or wrong, just a demonstration of how technology can be very helpful when used appropriately. When used inappropriately, it suffers from the same things any form of unresponsive and one-way communication suffers from: misinterpretation, escalation and lack of resolution. It is also to do with people's ease or discomfort with a form of communication. Some people relate very quickly to email communication, others less so. The ease and speed of email both enhance and can negatively escalate: group messages can be sent, when people may prefer to have things said more privately; unintended recipients; inappropriate recipients.

"MY HYSTERICAL BURDEN.'
"SHE'S HAVING A SYLVIA PLATH MOMENT......"

When you are experiencing any of these states, it is not a good time to send productive email.

And of course there is the world of dispersed teams: project communication; online facilitation; online work communities.

Robert Suler suggests that the Integration principle is hugely important in the development of successful online communities, for work or pleasure. That is making sure that the community becomes a part of people's whole lives and therefore has some perspective in a holistic way, rather than just in an Ethernet existence.

"...to be healthy and productive – for it [the community] to have 'staying' power – its members must integrate their online lives with their in-person lives. What does that mean? On the simplest level, it means they talk about their online experiences with the people they know offline, which will give them a clearer understanding of those experiences – especially if the online world is an ambiguous text-only or fantasy/avatar environment, where it's very easy to misinterpret other people's moods and intentions. Without the reality testing offered by one's friends and family, it's too easy to lose perspective, act out, and find oneself in a hurtful rather than enjoyable situation. When that happens too often to many people, the community can be destroyed.

'Integration' also means the members of a community contact each other offline, by telephone or meeting in-person. Face-to-face, they become familiar with each other's lives. Again, more reality testing and less acting out. As strong as online relationships can be, they are always made stronger when people meet in-person, when they commit to the intimacy of face-to-face encounters. While not everyone in the community can meet everyone else in-person, it is extremely helpful when there is a critical mass of people who have solidified their relationships offline. These people often become the stable, enduring core that hold the community together."

JO KIM (WWW.NAIMA.COM)
CONCLUDED THAT THERE ARE
NINE BASIC PRINCIPLES
FOR CREATING A COMMUNITY:

1. DEFINE THE PURPOSE OF THE COMMUNITY
2. CREATE DISTINCT GATHERING PLACES
3. CREATE MEMBER PROFILES THAT EVOLVE OVER TIME
4. PROMOTE EFFECTIVE LEADERSHIP
5. DEFINE A CLEAR-YET-FLEXIBLE CODE OF CONDUCT
6. ORGANIZE AND PROMOTE CYCLIC EVENTS
7. PROVIDE A RANGE OF ROLES THAT COUPLE POWER WITH RESPONSIBILITY
8. FACILITATE MEMBER-CREATED SUBGROUPS
9. INTEGRATE THE ONLINE ENVIRONMENT WITH THE "REAL" WORLD

CHOICE OVERLOAD

Does the wired world enable us or push us into roles? Who do we become in a wired world? If we assume a role, we have to suspend our freedom to act as the role requires. For example, a manager's words, actions and feelings belong to the role and not the person, although some people are so well cloaked that they make their "performance" believable even to themselves, overlooking any distinction between a manager's feelings and their own. *Is that positive or negative?* It is all down to the choice. *Have we freely chosen to view and interact with the world through this mask, whatever it may be? Is this a free suspension of our freedom?* If it is, we are inviting people to relate and react to us in a particular way. *If it isn't, what are we inviting, or being victim to?*

We can be playful with others when we engage at a level of choice, when there is no telling in advance where our relationship with them will come out, when no one has imposed an outcome on the relationship, apart from the decision to continue it.

"... YOU WILL KNOW THE TRUTH."
[JO.8.32]

Be careful what you wish for.......

"EVERY CHOICE BRINGS WITH IT A COST AND A PROMISE."
[VERNA DOZIER]

Having so much access to information does not define its veracity, or who is responsible for it. It does not seem as though we are ready to deal with the ethical and moral responsibilities that the Internet raises for us. Our need for speed and solutions just makes us press on faster in the hope that an answer will appear. It does not seem possible that anything or anyone would be able to stop the juggernaut from racing forward. Maybe the constructive future lies in our individual selves, to use the power appropriately and not expect anyone else to do it for us. Maybe that is too tough for you, particularly as you are so busy, and have very little time.....

".... PUBLIC JUDGMENT MAY BE SOUND AND MATURE, EVEN WISE, THOUGH ILL INFORMED. I HAVE LONG SUSPECTED THAT SOMETHING IS SERIOUSLY AMISS IN OUR CONVENTIONAL PARADIGM OF KNOWLEDGE WITH ITS RAZOR SHARP DISTINCTIONS BETWEEN 'OBJECTIVE' FACTS AND 'SUBJECTIVE' VALUES. IN REACHING ITS JUDGMENTS THROUGH DIALOGUE, THE PUBLIC IS HARKING BACK TO PRESCIENTIFIC WAYS OF KNOWING. THESE MAY ACTUALLY HAVE GREATER VALIDITY FOR THE IMPORTANT QUESTIONS OF LIVING TOGETHER THAN CURRENT THEORIES OF KNOWLEDGE."

[DON MICHAEL]

So what and where are the choice points? Often you avoid telling anyone you have made a decision for fear it is the wrong one, or it will go wrong, and you will be left with egg on your face. *Why do we find that such a terrifying thought?* Kids do things because they feel like it and are so concerned for their own survival and being that they worry less or protect themselves better. Kids, of course, totally underestimate their over-reactions because they're not yet aware of either. But we "teach" them the distinctions and… well… Reactions, over – and under –, are taught to be carefully managed. Fear of "anti-social" behaviour, e.g. over-reactions, keeps people a great distance from their own normal reactions and feelings. People, especially the so-called business types, learn early to avoid public reactions altogether and then forget that the choice was even there once, and made. Once the choice point is forgotten, it's like the little string pointing the way out of the deep dark cave is lost. *How do you recognize and use choice points?*

"TO BELIEVE
         IS TO KNOW YOU BELIEVE,
                     AND TO KNOW YOU BELIEVE
         IS NOT TO BELIEVE."

[JEAN-PAUL SARTRE]

The pace of relationships in the E world often forces, or is used as an excuse to force, the depth at which we relate to each other. *How much of that is real choice?*

What effect does it have on our ability to be playful and spontaneous? Paradoxically, playfulness with others is often the sign of a depth and trust in a relationship. It can also be a sign of a lack of investment in a relationship, as we may perceive there to be little risk in being playful in a relationship if there is nothing to lose….

"HE TREATS OBJECTS LIKE WOMEN."
[*THE BIG LEBOWSKI*]

BEYOND THE LOST HORIZON

People don't want to see new horizons; they want to go beyond them... We often speak of life and limiting our horizons. The horizon itself is not a reality, but a line beyond which we cannot see. There is always something beyond the horizon. Not being able to see or imagine is the real limitation. You only know where you are relative to a particular horizon; and you only know that by turning your back on it and seeing where you are. If you continually focus on one horizon, you have no sense of your relativity in the world. Making individual choices and ploughing your own furrow is pretty important and crucial to sense of choice, but if your own horizon is the only one you see, and you are ever pointed to that, you have limited both your vision and your chances of moving beyond it. Of course, only seeing other people's horizons has a similar limiting effect.

So many choices to make, at work and in your personal life. *On what do you base these choices? Is it partly about personal identity?* Who you are in the world, what and who are important to you. It isn't a one-time thing; as we evolve, our needs and expectations change; the inner being may not change dramatically (although that does happen for some), but the big question remains. The E world presents us with many options to be who we want to be. Sometimes the excessive choice is as overwhelming and stressful as being forced down a route we didn't want to travel. Cyberspace could be seen as an extension of your mind, a place to be stimulated and think things that might not have occurred to you. When you open that door, all sorts of fantasies and ideas can be projected on to the big computer screen. In its worse case, you could use this psychological space to vent or act out frustrations and anxieties. In the optimal case, you could use it as space to explore yourself as you engage with more people than you have ever been exposed to before.

CULTURAL TECHNOSOUP

So how does this differ across the globe? We talk about the World Wide Web, but just because the same data is accessible in Papua New Guinea as in New York, it doesn't mean that people approach the E world in the same way. Just because something is truly world-wide does not do away with cultural diversity. We may all access the same things, but we will want to do so in a different way; one that is in our framework, not another country's. We only buy ideas, or products or people if they make us feel good. Not only do we differ about the things that make us feel good as individuals, but also on a cultural basis.

Interestingly the cultural factors seem to override the technological factors in that they are more powerful in determining how people relate to each other. The technosoup that exists in California doesn't exist anywhere else in the same way. There are many other technological centres, but they don't operate in the same way. It is of course possible that the independent pioneer spirit that first brought people out here, the proximity of the centre of fantasy, Hollywood, the earthquake mentality, all contribute to the primordial technosoup. California as a land of the innovative, creative and just plain weird.

"That's what happens in the States: when suddenly something catches on, it balloons so out of control I think you burn out, you get destroyed. You may not get destroyed economically, you may become more famous and richer, but something dies." This was Terry Gilliam talking about how when people are starting a venture, business or creative, or both, the excitement and drive make you lose touch with the larger realities of the world. When that world wants a piece of your excitement and success, in America it wants to own and consume the excitement.

In the start-up world this could well describe the difference between the start-up group and those who want a piece of the action. It is at this point that many of the originators move on to create new ventures.

For example, the development of the Web took a very different course in the US from that in the UK and Europe. Most visuals in the US have their roots in selling and advertising. In the UK, many websites have their roots in club flyers. In the US, the Web is about sharing and advertising self and others. In the UK its early adopters used it to share secrets. For example, it was used to organize large groups of people to go to raves. It was fast and exclusive. It ensured that only people who were in the "webby club" would know and attend. It was always one step ahead of the police, so the party would be over by the time they had located the venue by more conventional means.

In Europe it seems that the semi-intellectual / art school / design culture with a punk attitude has used it to keep things "cool". They actually don't want just anyone to find "it" on the Web; only those who are part of the cognoscenti. Some sites are geared to put off the average surfer.... try hell.com.... It seems that the European attraction is more to do with cool, exclusivity and belonging to a club, rather than the US attraction which wants to create huge communities that go to the widest possible group. Big is more beautiful than exclusivity or cool. Neither of these approaches is right or wrong, but in terms of E commerce and both capturing and maintaining relationships, these elements need to be thought through. They may not affect mainstream shoppers, but they will have an impact on some areas.

We can see some of these motivational differences in the story of the motor car. The car was invented and built in Europe. It was built for racing and/or for someone else to drive. It was kept elitist. The US invention was not the car; it was mass production of the car. Take it to the largest common denominator. It's not socialism; it's blanket; just like the Web.

So are there any common factors that link those who seem to thrive in the virtual world:

$\rightarrow$ ENERGY
$\rightarrow$ BELIEF AND CONFIDENCE IN WHAT THEY ARE DOING
$\rightarrow$ DRIVE AND DETERMINATION
$\rightarrow$ DESIRE TO FIND NEW WAYS OF DOING THINGS

It could well be that the energy, confidence and drive are what actually drive these organizations. It is not dissimilar to the bond between climbing partners. You have to know and trust your partner totally. There is usually no time to think or check out. You just have to believe and do. Start-ups work this way. Sometimes it is a couple of driven pals who believe and want to make their dream happen. This pushes them to try new things, to boldly go and to be the first. That excitement has to be shared, otherwise the buzz doesn't get regenerated, and when the going gets tough, people lose faith. Like climbers, when the going gets tough, these guys look into themselves and each other and find that something extra that gets them "to the top". Again similarly to climbers, many of these bright young things are not very social animals, but share extraordinary faith and closeness with the people they go into business with. It's a very special partnership.

These attributes seem to be common whether the E venture is in Kuala Lumpur, London or San Francisco. Once people start using words like risk-taker, creative and innovative, the cultures invest the words with their interpretations.....

Well, people already seem to be fed up with being treated as commodities, potential buyers. They are fed up of working for and with people who treat them as if they don't exist. A medium such as the Internet holds such promise to connect, inform and challenge, and at the same time abuses its audience by treating them solely as consumers. Our demand for instant gratification and quick, risk-free return on investment, financial or otherwise, leaves no time for intricate things to be worked out. No time to evaluate true value and worth, no willingness to listen or be patient. Sometimes an Internet relationship allows you more control than you have in real life, and is therefore very attractive.

No right or wrong.

What is it that you seek in relationships that will enrich your life, and/or increase your satisfaction and effectiveness at work? Answering this question is at the heart of defining how you operate to get the best from self, colleagues, business and personal relationships.

"ALL I CAN SAY IS THAT THE HUMAN SPECIES IS ASTONISHING. IT IS, AFTER ALL, A SPECIES THAT HAS TRANSFORMED ITS HABITAT COMPLETELY. NO OTHER SPECIES HAS A COMPARABLE RECORD. YOU CAN NEVER TELL WHERE THESE LITTLE BASTARDS ARE GOING TO TAKE YOU, THESE HUMAN BEINGS: THEIR ASTONISHING SUBTLETY, THEIR INTELLIGENCE — THEIR PERVERSITY, EVEN, WHICH IS OFTEN A PERVERSITY OF GENIUS. IT'S TRUE THAT WE ARE SURROUNDED BY DUMBBELLS. BUT IN THE END, THE GENIUSES TAKE CHARGE OF REALITY."

[SAUL BELLOW]

"WE'RE SO WELL INFORMED
                      THAT WE'VE LOST
ALL SENSE OF MEANING.
              WE KNOW THE PRICE OF EVERYTHING,
                          BUT WE'VE LOST
ALL SENSE OF VALUE."

[CHARACTER IN *DISTRACTION*, BY BRUCE STERLING]

[PACE]
AND RELATIONSHIPS

MOORE IS LESS?
TRAVEL AT WARP SPEED
E-LLUSION OF CONTROL
NOWHERE TO RUN, NOWHERE TO HIDE
E=MC3
PRESENT TENSE, FUTURE IMPERFECT
E COSTS, E OPPORTUNITIES
ECONOMIES OF SOUL
WHO'S DRIVING THIS TRAIN?

"FRIDAY THEY ASKED YOU TO TAKE THE COMPANY ONLINE.
MONDAY, THEY ASKED YOU TO BUILD LONG-LASTING
PERSONALIZED RELATIONSHIPS WITH ALL YOUR CUSTOMERS.
TODAY THEY ASKED IF YOU WERE DONE YET."

[ADVERT FOR VIGNETTE.COM]

"I DON'T SEE A DIFFERENCE BETWEEN WORK AND PLAY – IT'S JUST LIFE."
[WOMAN IN CHARGE OF ETRADE]

"THE WORLD
        IS FULL OF PEOPLE

                WHO DON'T KNOW
                    WHERE THEY'RE GOING

AND WANT TO GET THERE
　　　　TOO FAST...."

[TAXI DRIVER IN *THE BISHOP'S WIFE*]

"BETWEEN IMPULSE AND ACTION
THERE IS A REALM BEGGING FOR YOUR ATTENTION."

[HOLODOCTOR IN *VOYAGER*]

ONCE...

[UNKNOWN]

GOD

CREATED

TIME

SO

THAT

EVERYTHING

WOULDN'T

HAPPEN

AT

ONCE...

[UNKNOWN]

The most talked about manifestation of the E world is its pace. *Where does that come from, and how does it impact on relationships? How many times and examples of how fast the pace is now do you need to know?*

MOORE IS LESS?

Gordon E Moore, co-founder of Intel, was responsible in his early career for Moore's Law. It states that the number of transistors on a chip, and hence the cost-effectiveness of computers, essentially doubles every 18 months. This is an exponential law and breaks down cities and concentrations of power, as small, cheap, distributed organizations and indicates that under those circumstances, technologies are likely to prevail.

> "IT [INFORMATION TECHNOLOGY] SHOWS EVERY SIGN OF CONSTANT ACCELERATION UNTIL AT LEAST 2015;
> 37 DOUBLINGS, ABOUT A 137-BILLIONFOLD INCREASE OF POWER IN 56 YEARS. THERE IS NO PRECEDENT
> IN THE HISTORY OF TECHNOLOGY FOR THE SUSTAINED SELF-FEEDING GROWTH OF COMPUTER CAPABILITY."
>
> **[STEWART BRAND]**

As the continuous revolutions in the computer industry have kept up and increased the pace, new machines are obsolete after three years. Stewart Brand describes how the digitizing of communications via the Internet spawned Metcalfe's Law, named after Xerox engineer Bob Metcalfe. It states that the power of a network grows as the square of the number of users (people or devices on the Net. Hence the explosion of the Web in the mid 1990s, when the Net's total content was doubling every 100 days. He describes how Metcalfe's Law explains why 50 million people had to get on the Internet in just a few years:

"THE AGGREGATE VALUE OF OTHER USERS WAS SO GREAT THAT THEY COULD NOT AFFORD TO MISS THE BOAT."

In most systems that humans design, anything matching this rate of increase would mean catastrophe. Imagine a motorway with 40 times as many cars, or Windows with 40 times as many lines of code. Everything about the emerging role of the Internet, our reliance on it for communication and information and the idea that we might store data there rather than on local machines, might be very different if it were constantly failing, falling behind schedule, or behaving like many of our other creations. Widespread theft of credit card numbers, the sale of intercepted personal data to terrorists and botched prescriptions from online pharmacies leading to drug reactions would all have dramatically changed the perception of the Internet. We do seem to trust it...The fact that it has worked and not failed spectacularly may also have led us to the conclusion that the faster we go, the more we will achieve...

"THE MANAGEMENT OF Y2K COUPLED WITH THE NORMAL FAILURE WE'VE SIMPLY COME TO EXPECT DEMONSTRATED TO ME THAT PERHAPS MANKIND HAS CROSSED SOME SORT OF THRESHOLD THAT WILL MAKE OUR RELATIONSHIPS WITH MACHINES MUCH MORE INTIMATE. WE SEEM TO TRUST THEM NOW AND BELIEVE THAT, DESPITE THEIR SHORTCOMINGS, THEY ARE ULTIMATELY GOOD AND WILL ULTIMATELY DO THE RIGHT THING; A KIND OF BLIND FAITH RESERVED NORMALLY FOR DEITY AND THOSE OF OUR SPECIES."

[BRUCE STERLING]

Is it because it has become such an everyday part of our lives that we don't have the fascination that we have with other industries? Interestingly, people don't picket Internet or related companies. I wonder why the protestors at the World Trade Organization conference in Seattle, who threw rocks at Niketown, did not call Jeff Bezos and ask how it felt to know that his Amazon stock was worth more than the total assets of the bottom 30 million US families combined. It seems that the big "engines" of accumulation – software, communications and the Internet – are significant for the backlash they haven't provoked. Yet. *So does this "trust" we have in the E world entice us to travel at a faster pace than we can actually go?*

"IN A WORLD THAT CAN'T WAIT 24 HOURS FOR A PACKAGE,
THERE'S A PLACE THAT STILL WAITS 18 YEARS FOR A WHISKY."
[ADVERT FOR GLENLIVET]

TRAVEL AT WARP SPEED

One ad agency was being almost harassed by potential .com clients who were so concerned that Christmas this year would make or break them, that they were phoning up asking to get advertising space with a week's notice.....everything they want, they want now.

There seems to be no space for planning or thinking ahead. As Richard Stagg remarked, "The one thing I have lost is my time to reflect and think." The impact of this is startling and, not surprisingly, does not actually save or create time. It only creates stressed and pressurized people who find it even harder to know and find what they seek, because they are so pressured. *If this is so blindingly obvious and not rocket science, why do people do it? What makes us desirous of operating at warp speed, when we only have impulse engines?*

The effects of travelling at warp speed are many... (and warped...):

DISORIENTATION, DISSATISFACTION, DYSFUNCTION, TO NAME BUT A FEW.

The faster you go, the faster you want to go. You can never go fast enough.

It is also incredibly difficult to tell someone at warp speed that this is not making them happy, and is not good for their health. Robert Sapolsky tells of the time he was being interviewed by a magazine about his views on stress. All was going well until the interviewer asked him about how he personally dealt with stress. He responded by saying that he loved his work, worked out every day and had a fabulous marriage. The interviewer blew up at him saying she couldn't write about how wonderful his marriage was, as many of her readers were 45-year-old professionals who were unlikely ever to get married, and they wanted to hear that that is ok and how wonderful that was. It was like telling a Rwandan refugee to be careful about their chocolate and saturated fat intake. This sense of dissatisfaction is what keeps people driving the pace; to find that elusive "something": the ultimate product, the ultimate sale, the ultimate deal.

"THE FIRST THING YOU LEARN
                          IS YOU ALWAYS GOTTA

WAIT."

[WILLIAM BURROUGHS]

"YOU ARE EXPERIENCING SPIRITUAL
EMPTINESS BECAUSE YOUR POWER HAS ISOLATED YOU FROM OTHER
HUMAN BEINGS."

[LISA SIMPSON]

"POWER IS THE WILL TO DO WHAT THE OTHER GUY WON'T."

[*THE USUAL SUSPECTS*]

"IS THE LORD OF THE UNIVERSE IN?"

[*HIS GIRL FRIDAY*]

E-LLUSION OF CONTROL

So this feeling of dissatisfaction that forces the pace does not make people happy, or more effective at their work. In fact it seems to make them feel as if they have lost control of their lives and how they live them. In a desperate bid to feel more comfortable, sometimes people give themselves the illusion of control by keeping up. *What is it you want to control? Who really sets the pace? What would be happening differently for you if you felt in control?*

"MANY PEOPLE SEEM TO FEEL THAT CHANGE IN ONE'S SELF CONCEPT CAN COME ABOUT SMOOTHLY. THIS IS NOT TRUE IN ANY PERSON...WHEN WE LEARN SOMETHING SIGNIFICANT ABOUT OURSELVES AND ACT ON THAT NEW LEARNING, THAT STARTS A WAVE OF CONSEQUENCES WE CAN NEVER FULLY APPRECIATE."

[CARL ROGERS]

When people get hooked on the E wave, it does not appear as though they are caught up knowingly. They use phrases like "swept along" and "overwhelmed". Everyone is on a learning curve but seems to have forgotten that on a learning curve, new things happen. Speed does not make the new things happen faster. That is one of the E-llusions....

The average British executive receives 190 messages a day, including 48 phone calls, 23 external emails, 20 letters, 15 internal emails, 13 post-it notes, 12 message slips, 11 voicemail messages, 11 faxes, 8 mobile phone calls, 3 express postal deliveries, 2 pager messages, and 3 courier deliveries. Four out of ten are interrupted every 10 minutes.

Ok, you can do what you want with these numbers, but there is no denying the pace and quantity of the information age. Information anxiety gets created by the gap between what we know and what we could know. It is a losing battle: a daily newspaper contains more information than the average person was likely to come across in a lifetime in the 17th century. Marshall McLuhan suggested that we should only read left-hand pages in publications, as we had too much information. He wasn't referring to Web pages either.

Increased degrees of predictability and information are not always helpful: it does not help to get information about common events, because they are basically inevitable, or about very rare events, because you weren't scared of them in the first place. It doesn't reduce stress to get information a few seconds before something bad happens, because there isn't time to derive the psychological advantages of being able to relax, or way in advance of the event, because there's no need to worry, it's so far away and may never happen. Y2K was a good example of the latter; knowing that there was a problem did not decrease anxiety, partly because the knowing was not enough. Once you know, you want to take it away or control it.

Sometimes that little bit of extra knowledge makes us more anxious rather than less. For example, if you were going in to see your boss, and just before you went in, someone said, "Hey, a word to the wise: he is in a bad mood today, and is out for blood..." Well, most people would be more anxious with that data, although maybe less surprised. All of the available information taunts us with how out of control we feel; stupid, out of touch and overwhelmed.

Alternatively too much of a sense of control is just as debilitating whether the sense is accurate or not. Not only may you have further to fall, but when the sense of control is illusory – as in you can never catch up, but "If I just work four more hours I will be closer" – it is anything but psychologically comforting to believe you can control the uncontrollable. It is an intellectual exercise, which isn't even logical.

Sherman James, an epidemiologist at the University of Michigan, describes this "pathogenic" illusion of control as "John Henryism". This refers to an American hero who tried to outpace a steam drill tunnelling through a mountain by hammering a six-foot-long steel drill. Well, he did beat the machine, and then fell dead from the effort. Sherman James defines John Henryism as the belief that any and all demands can be conquered and delivered, so long as you work hard enough. On questionnaires, John Henry individuals say things like, "When things don't go the way I want them, it just makes me work even harder." Or "Once I make up my mind to do something, I stay with it until the job is completely done." These are people with what is called an internal locus of control. They believe that with enough determination and effort, they can control all outcomes. *How many John Henrys do you know?*

You might ask, "What is the problem with that?" In many cases, particularly middle-class, well-educated individuals, particularly in the United States, attributing results in life to your own efforts is not only valued, but revered. What it doesn't address is the impact this has on relationships: if you are the only one responsible for the effort and outcome, you exclude and diminish others in all parts of your life, private and professional. You also make yourself all-powerful.... *what happens to the all-powerful when they fail?*

"THE HARDER THEY COME, THE HARDER THEY FALL, ONE AND ALL."
[JIMMY CLIFF]

In a bigger picture, where does this leave the could-have-beens or less privileged, who end up with the "If only I could have worked harder....." This frequently manifests itself in heart disease and hypertension.

In the workplace, it results in unreal deadlines, demotivation and high stress levels which lead to an inability to think creatively or be innovative (with either problems or new ways of working). A swift reality check on what is really important, what you need to achieve and what people are spending their time on, helps maintain perspective and regain focus without slowing the pace.

"ALL SAIL, NO RUDDER."
[LORD BYRE]

A lot of this has to do with being aware, responsive and accepting. This list does not include defensiveness. This is not compatible with any relationship, let alone connectivity. In a more turbulent and ambiguous future you need to free yourself from the notion that you know exactly what you are doing and exactly how to do it, without losing awareness and drive. This not only allows for mistakes without blame, it allows us to be creative and responsive to situations. That is not possible when you are on the defensive. Once you have started a defence routine, you end up repeating behaviour. If you do what you have always done, you get what you always got.

"PEOPLE SEEMED TO BE MUCH MORE EFFECTIVE WHEN THEY GAVE UP THE ILLUSION OF BEING IN CONTROL, AND INSTEAD TRIED TO WORK THINGS THROUGH WITH OTHERS. WHEN THEY HELD ONTO THE NEED TO DEAL ONLY WITH WHAT WAS UNDER THEIR CONTROL, THEY WEREN'T VERY EFFECTIVE. THEY OPERATED IN AN ALL-OR-NOTHING, BLACK-OR-WHITE, WIN-OR-LOSE WORLD THAT DIDN'T REFLECT THE WAY THE WORLD REALLY WORKS. THE SOUTH AFRICANS, BY CONTRAST, WERE PLAYING IN A GREY ZONE BETWEEN COMPLETE CONTROL ON THE ONE HAND AND NO INFLUENCE ON THE OTHER: A 'GENERATIVE DOMAIN' WHERE THEY HAD LESS CONTROL THAN THEY WISHED BUT MORE INFLUENCE THAN THEY EXPECTED."
[ADAM KAHANE COMMENTING ON DISCUSSIONS ON THE FUTURE OF SOUTH AFRICA]

Martin Luther said that we should pray and work. *Ora et labora.* Just doing work was a positive action in itself, whatever the nature of the work.

Richard Reeves describes six different types of what he calls workaholics, whose desire to work stems from different places. They all existed before the E world. They just ramp up their pace in the E world, or it enables them to push their own particular pacing even further.

ERGOPHILES:
THEY LOVE THEIR JOBS AND THEIR WORK. THEY TRULY LIVE TO WORK, EVEN THOUGH IT ROBS THEM OF EVERYTHING ELSE. IF THEIR HEALTH FAILS OR THEY LOSE THEIR JOBS, THEIR LIVES LOSE ALL MEANING AND THEY CEASE TO FUNCTION.
EXAMPLE: GORDON BROWN
NEIL KINNOCK ONCE SAID OF THIS DRIVEN MAN, "GET GORDON BROWN A HOBBY OR A WIFE."

ACHIEVERS:
THIS GROUP MAY HAVE BEEN AIDED AND ABETTED IN THEIR YOUTH BY THEIR PARENTS IN STRIVING TO EVER GREATER ACHIEVEMENTS. THEY NEED TO BE CONSTANTLY RECOGNIZED FOR WHAT THEY HAVE DONE, BY EITHER PROMOTION OR PUBLICITY, AND ARE USUALLY PRISONERS OF THEIR OWN PERFECTIONISM.
EXAMPLE: ANNIE LIEBOWITZ
HER LONG CAREER HAS SPANNED A QUARTER OF A CENTURY, AND SHE HAS CONSTANTLY PUSHED TO BETTER HER LAST PHOTOGRAPH AND STAY WITH THE ERA SHE IS PHOTOGRAPHING.

POWER MAD:
THESE INDIVIDUALS ARE ADDICTED TO THE IDEA OF EVERYTHING DEPENDING ON AND FLOWING FROM THEM. THEY WILL DO ANYTHING TO GET AND KEEP POWER. THEY ARE UNLIKELY TO GET THIS LEVEL OF POWER IN ANY AREA OF THEIR LIVES OTHER THAN WORK, E.G. FAMILY. FALLING OFF THIS PERCH IS VERY BRUISING.
EXAMPLE: MARGARET THATCHER
SHE KNEW WHAT EVERYONE WAS DOING, HAD ENORMOUS AMOUNTS OF ZEALOUS, FOCUSED ENERGY, AND DOMINATED HER CABINET, GOVERNMENT AND THE COUNTRY.

MORTALLY COILED:
THOSE WHO SHARE THIS IDEAL FEEL COMPELLED TO MAKE THEIR MARK BEFORE THEY DIE. JUST AS MOZART CONTINUED WRITING UNTIL HE DIED, THEY NEED TO PRODUCE BEFORE IT IS TOO LATE. OFTEN DEPRESSED, THEY FIND IT HARD TO ACCEPT PRAISE.
EXAMPLE: NORMAN COOK AKA FATBOY SLIM
"... NOT HAVING TIME FOR MY FRIENDS AND BASICALLY PISSING EVERYONE OFF. I WAS TAKEN OVER BY THE JOB..." HIS GP REFERRED HIM TO A THERAPIST "TO SEE IF I WAS MAD. I WASN'T. I WAS UNHAPPY."

FAMILY FIRST-ERS:
THESE WORKERS ONLY TAKE SUCCESS IF IT FITS IN WITH CHILDREN'S BIRTHDAYS AND BEDTIMES AND /OR THEIR PERSONAL PASTIMES. THEY ARE USUALLY DELIGHTED TO HAVE SUCCEEDED, BUT WOULD HAVE BEEN HAPPY TO FALL SLIGHTLY SHORT OF THEIR PRESENT POSITION.
EXAMPLE: GERRY ROBINSON, CHAIRMAN OF THE FORTE GROUP
HE IS PROUD TO GO HOME EARLY AND WORKS IN CONCENTRATED BURSTS.

PLEASURE SEEKERS:
THIS GROUP ENJOY THEIR WORK, BUT FIND THAT OTHER ACTIVITIES BRING THEM MORE PLEASURE. THEY WORK TO LIVE, EVEN THOSE WHO END UP IN ENVIABLE JOBS. OFTEN THEIR RELAXED CHARM LANDS THEM JOBS THAT HIGH ACHIEVERS WOULD KILL FOR.
EXAMPLE: KENNETH CLARKE
AS CHANCELLOR, HE WAS APPALLED AT THE LONG-HOURS CULTURE AT THE TREASURY. TO COUNTER THIS HE ISSUED STRICT GUIDELINES FOR WORK TO BE COMPLETED. HE OFTEN LURED MINISTERIAL COLLEAGUES TO RONNIE SCOTT'S AFTER A LATE NIGHT SITTING. "THE KIND OF DISORGANIZED LIFESTYLE OF JAZZ PEOPLE, THE LATE NIGHTS, THE STRANGE VENUES, THE APPROACH TO LIFE. I ENJOY IT."

"IT'S BETTER TO BURN OUT

THAN FADE AWAY."

[NEIL YOUNG]

There is both danger and seduction in an all-consuming occupation, and there is no doubt that it gives you meaning for a time, but it may not be the whole of you. It is that lack of wholeness, paradoxically called empty, which many of these people feel. *Why am I working so hard, doing something I believe in, and I still feel something is missing?*

> "WE HAVE MASSIVE FLOWS OF INFORMATION AND CAPITAL, BUT WE HAVE A GRAVE SCARCITY OF MEANING. WE KNOW WHAT WE CAN BUY, BUT WE DON'T KNOW WHAT WE WANT."
>
> [BRUCE STERLING]

NOWHERE TO RUN, NOWHERE TO HIDE

There is a saying that men trained in the winter to win their wars in the summer. When I mentioned this to a young E-commerce turk, he replied, "I foresee a continuous winter training period and little chance of a relaxing or even winning summer."

The lack of seasons is a fact of life in California, but it is almost a metaphor for the pace people take their work/life. They describe their lives as spontaneous and quick to adapt, but they are also driven by events which seem to have no space between them or distinguishing marks or memories. Everything seems to meld into one, and that gives the impression of an even faster pace as it seems relentless. There are few breaks even in the day. Often people who take lunch breaks are regarded as slackers, and it certainly is something out of the ordinary to take one. If you talk to any E CEO, they pretty much all say that the thing they can't get over is the speed.

> "YOU'RE DRIVING TOO FAST – YOU FEEL THE EXHILARATION AND THE THREAT – YOU MUST TURN LEFT AND RIGHT AT DEATH-DEFYING SPEED WITHOUT BLINKING – NEVER BLINK IF YOU GO UP AND DOWN WITH THE NEWS, YOU'LL NEVER MAKE IT....YOU HAVE TO BE DEADLY, BRUTALLY HONEST WITH YOURSELF AND OTHERS BECAUSE IF YOU LET A REAL PROBLEM FESTER A DAY OR TWO, YOU'LL SEE SOMEONE IN YOUR REAR-VIEW MIRROR COMING AFTER YOU."
>
> [ROGER SIBONT, CEO OF EPIPHANY]

JoMei Chang, from Vitria Technology, says, "There's no place to hide. It forces you to be on your toes every minute, every second." E CEOs will tell you that that is why they carry every electronic business device: cell phone, two-way pager, Palm Pilot, laptop. Sounds like that increases the pace; the more accessible you are the more likely people will put the pressure on you. *What would actually happen if you were out of contact for an hour? What would you miss? Who would miss you? Who would get one up on you? Is it all about getting there first?* In the E world, these questions are hard to answer, because there is nothing there. As Gertrude Stein said of Oakland, "There is no there there. Nothing tangible. It's pure mind." Tim Koogle, CEO of Yahoo, says – "There's nothing physical - it's all intangible. I love it." *Is this the ultimate Emperor's new clothes?*

ENERGY = MOVING AND CHANGE CHARISMA CHALLENGE
MAKING THE EARTH MOVE....
SEISMIC INTERACTIONS......

E=MC3

Of course, every new challenge needs those people at the vanguard to drive through newness and the uncomfortable. Quite often these people are visionary and charismatic, and have a wonderful, inspiring story to tell. People want to be part of their story. That can be a part of the problem: *you can become part of that person's story* – as opposed to the story itself. The trick is to involve people in the story itself, not just recounting the tale. One of the things the E world can do is let many people have access to the story, so more feel part of it. The excitement keeps up the pace, and also people's desire not to fall behind, or let their leaders down.

"YOU'VE GOT TO EVANGELIZE THE CONCEPT."
[JOHN CHAMBERS, CEO OF CISCO SYSTEMS]

Michael Dell says he has found a foolproof way to spot an E CEO: "Does he or she get bandwidth separation anxiety? That is, do they get crazy when deprived of high speed connection to the rest of the planet?......It happens to me. You kinda get the shakes." Sounds like an addiction to me...

FORTUNE MAGAZINE LISTED
THE COMPARATIVE SKILLS NEEDED
BY E CEOS TO SURVIVE THE PACE....

TRADITIONAL CEO	E CEO
ENCOURAGING	EVANGELIZING
ALERT	PARANOID
CORDIAL	BRUTALLY FRANK
INFOTECH SEMI-LITERATE (AT BEST)	INFOTECH LITERATE (AT LEAST)
CLEARLY FOCUSED	INTENSELY FOCUSED
FAST MOVING	FASTER MOVING
HATES AMBIGUITY	LIKES AMBIGUITY
SUFFERS FROM TECHNOLOGY- CONFRONTATION ANXIETY	SUFFERS FROM BANDWIDTH- SEPARATION ANXIETY
A PARAGON OF GOOD JUDGEMENT	A PARAGON OF GOOD JUDGEMENT
AGE: 57	AGE: 38
RICH	REALLY RICH

In a way all the differences are pace-driven, or at least about intensity of pace. It's not just the ability to visualize a different future; it's about being passionate about it. You are making decisions on much less data than before, and that cuts both ways; you get faster decisions, but with less thought for verification and its potential impact. The level of risk tolerance is much higher, with a need to let go of issues in an environment where many things are unknowable.

You always have to provide a great place to work, or else people will just move on down the road; those with the skills can go anywhere.

Their dynamism and the force of the pace make people think that they are all "on the same page"; the reality is that they are not. They are just all travelling very fast, sometimes not even in the same direction. They don't even make the time to check each other out. The chances of the desired collaboration are therefore slim to zero. Everything is in the moment – people have to knee-jerk to any call that comes up; it is hard not to take the calls. Some of them are real and urgent. *When does it get used as an excuse?* It makes everything and everyone Now. If you aren't now, you lose. If everything and everyone is now, then no one has any special value or importance. Keeping up is the only value. *What will be the long-term effect of a community that has keeping up as its overriding value?*

PRESENT TENSE, FUTURE IMPERFECT

People who become stressed by the idea of keeping up tend to fall into two camps: those who are driven by visions of success, and those who are driven by a fear of failure. Both of these end up in dysfunctional relationships, both personally and professionally. I wonder if human beings were actually made to have the constant adrenaline rush with no time for thought. *If that were true, would we need all the brain cells we have and the enormous capacity we have to think about both things and people?*

Certainly the word "overwhelmed" appears in most conversations with people whose lives revolve around the E globe. It seems very hard for them to think of anything other than real time. Their sense of future is poor, and there seems to be a permanent sense of impermanence.

> "IF YOU BRING FORTH WHAT IS WITHIN YOU, WHAT YOU BRING FORTH WILL SAVE YOU. IF YOU DO NOT BRING FORTH WHAT IS WITHIN YOU, THEN WHAT YOU DO NOT BRING FORTH WILL DESTROY YOU."
>
> [THOMAS, FROM THE GNOSTIC GOSPELS]

If all your energy is focused on the present, what do you have left for the future?

They all seem agreed on one thing: there is no way to keep up. That would seem to be one hell of an indictment for a society. Everyone is set to fail. This competition among individuals, perceived or otherwise, leads to more frustration and rage with the unfairness of life; so frequently this leads to a "I'm gonna get mine, you're on your own, buddy, in fact up yours", and this just continues to feed a very unvirtuous circle.

"IT'S DOG EAT DOG AND VICE VERSA."
[FRED ALLEN]

Gloomy, huh? Well, for everyone except ADD adults, who seem to thrive in this culture. ADD is Attention Deficiency Disorder. Children who have this have very short attention spans and are sometimes referred to as "hyperactive". For the speeded-out guys and gals of Silicon Valley, there appears to be no societal Ritalin to calm them down and give them perspective and balance. (Ritalin is a drug prescribed for ADD sufferers to enable them to be in the world.)

Wherever you sit in the world, consumer, developer, customer, observer, creator, we have never really experienced before being forced to connect at such a pace. The triteness of saying "Everything is changing" and "Things move so fast nowadays" sometimes allows us to avoid dealing with the changes.

E COSTS, E OPPORTUNITIES

One way of illustrating this is to look at the impact on our personal lives. One individual told me how much pleasure and relaxation they got from working out, but they didn't feel they could do yoga because it was too slow. *Are these situations discrete, and individual, or are they a permanent and pervasive way of being? In which case, how do you find appropriate outlets for frustration and means of social support in difficult times?* One thing is for certain, it isn't about control. Well, not control as we may consider it.

THE ONLY WAY TO STAY IN CONTROL IS TO LET GO.

If you look at this from the other way, the opportunities for self-realization have never been as plentiful. There is a difficult line to walk between individualistic and being selfish. Sometimes it's hard to see the line; sometimes we cross it unknowingly. We have still crossed it, and part of getting grounded is knowing when your need to be "whole" and "be all you can be" is not damaging anything or anyone else. It is also very hard to be an individual and feel as though people will still accept you in a world which is in transition from being conformist and controlled to being ok with people doing their own thing. That takes a great deal of courage, faith, bananas and yogurt.

In terms of Pace in the E world, it means it is hard to be the first one who says "That deadline is totally unrealistic, and has to be shifted"; or, "I am going away this weekend, and my personal time is crucial to my ability to function effectively at work so I will not come into work this weekend." Quite often, those that do are regarded with envy by those who were not courageous enough to take the risk, but display the envy with comments like, "Oh, so you don't care about the rest of the team, then." Most pioneers of a new way of being were often regarded as marginals or outcasts by their society. They then tended to seek out their psychographic companions, rather than their demographic ones.

Simon was a very bright and successful self-employed software designer/consultant. He had worked for himself for over 12 years, and had a reputation for being very intuitive, quick and to the point. Unfortunately, he was sometimes too close to the point for some of his larger corporate clients, and said things that they didn't want to hear. This made them very uncomfortable, although they seemed to know he was right in his assessments. He had many outside interests and was very good at protecting his free time.

He would often work very long, intense hours so that he could get a long break. That was his choice, but many of his friends found his freedom to choose intimidating. It would only be displayed by comments like "Oh, typical consultant", but Simon grew less and less comfortable with the fact that many of his friends were feeling desperately overwhelmed with the pace of the E world, yet he had made his choices and was at peace with them. What he had become uncomfortable with was the fact that he did not feel able to say he was happy as it felt smug. He began to feel guilty about being grounded and started to either retreat or dumb himself down. He went abroad on an assignment, and met up with a group of people who seemed to appreciate his way of being; he felt free to be who he was, and consequently found new levels of creativity. He spent more and more time with his new "tribe", and eventually took up a contract that allowed him to do that. He had changed his pace, but the people around him were uncomfortable with it.

However well you know yourself, there is always more to reach. When you are under the gun to produce, you can actually become more open and sensitive to possibility, because of the pressure. You are so in need that opportunities for like-minded being and enjoyment can be heightened. This is the other side to the dark intensity of pace, where the pressure stops you seeing what is around you.

Sometimes the only way we get to see this is through relationships with other people. If you withdraw when under pressure, it's the pressure you feel. If you can find someone who resonates on your frequency, not only can you release the tension, but you see things you might not see in an unheightened state. The pace and intensity of the E world bring with them tremendous opportunities; how you perceive them and respond to them is what creates pressure or excitement.

ECONOMIES OF SOUL

Pace seems to stop feeling like a pressure whenever you stop seeing everything as a goal, or seeing people as objects.

People do not enjoy being treated as commodities or nameless, faceless individuals. We all warm to someone who calls us by our name, even when you call up Amazon.com and it addresses you by your name. We all desire to be accepted for who we are. Within an organization, that means really tapping into the source of feelings and fantasy, emotion and imagination. Whatever you are selling, whether it is an idea, yourself or an electric kettle, the only reason people will buy is if it makes them feel good. The art of persuasion is embedded in that premise. People who are effective at persuading or influencing others understand what feeling good would look like for the person they want to influence, not to themselves. They know this by observing and asking questions of the person they want to affect. When they feel they have understood their need, they then sell whatever it is they want to sell, but Only In The Other Person's Framework. They understand what is important emotionally to that person, and frame what they say appropriately. Feelings and fantasy are often where this feelgood emotion resides. Sometimes you don't know how to word it, but a skilful person can help. This is something that is hard to do on the Internet. You cannot see or pick up verbal clues, and it is hard to get enough emotional data. So much of the time you guess. Often the guess will be in your image, not theirs.

Also, in the better informed consumer world of E commerce, reason and logic do not provide a competitive advantage as everyone has them or access to them. Many people give value for money or pay good salaries. Successful E companies want to keep both their employees and their customers inspired and excited. They know it makes sense; but knowing is not always doing, and sometimes the demon Pace obstructs the surprise. The authors of *Funky Business* call this "Economies of Soul".

"AS ALBERTO ALESSI, FOUNDER OF THE COMPANY WITH THE SAME NAME, ONCE SAID, 'PEOPLE HAVE AN ENORMOUS NEED FOR ART AND POETRY THAT INDUSTRY DOES NOT YET UNDERSTAND.' AS ALESSI CHARGES SOME $80 FOR A TOILET BRUSH, HE MUST BE DOING SOMETHING RIGHT. THERE IS MONEY IN EMOTION."

[*FUNKY BUSINESS*]

Not everyone wants to be touched emotionally in the same way, but the danger for E commerce is that it creates expectations of a relationship that will touch emotions when it has no intention of doing so.

"BELIEVE IN YOURSELF."

[ADVERT FOR AMERITRADE, AN ONLINE TRADING SERVICE]

However, if the success of E business rests on its ability to leverage talent and knowledge in the fastest, most appropriate way, then an understanding of relationships is crucial. Announcing you have no time for them does not make them happen. It needn't slow things down, if it becomes a way of being, but it will change the pace from being punishing to fast.

"THE IMPOSSIBLE BECOMES POSSIBLE, BECAUSE MORE OF YOURSELF IS AVAILABLE."

[CAROL MONTGOMERY]

We talk about expanding physical bandwidth to meet the demands of the Internet; we need to expand our emotional bandwidth to be able to cope with the possibilities that the E world presents us with. It is available to everyone.

"I'M USED TO WORKING WITH PEOPLE WITH A FUSE UP THEIR BEHIND."

[SILICON VALLEY CONSULTANT]

"I AM ENOUGH."
[CARL ROGERS]

WHO'S DRIVING THIS TRAIN?

Unfortunately, people really don't believe this statement. Visible achievement, accumulation and knowledge are seen as the key indicators of an individual's value in the E world. *Why can't it be enough? Why is it not possible for us to see the abundance of information and opportunities of connection as ways for us to be, as opposed to an end in itself?*

It seems as though in an extreme example of John Henryism, we believe that although technology could make our lives simpler, we still have to look as though we are working hard, otherwise we don't deserve it. It's too easy.

The pace of technology has outstripped the pace of relationships; in order to catch up, we need to be aware of how to catch up, where the gaps are, where our capacities are, what we are utilizing well, and what is being abused. *Yes, we still can improve and progress, but what is the hurry? Who are we racing with?* Freedom exists when you avoid trying to run with the technological pack. Everybody has software.

> "YOU CAN'T FIND THE LEADING EDGE BECAUSE THE STAMPEDE HAS TRAMPLED OVER IT."
> [UNKNOWN]

The propeller of pace creates a wake and backlash for both self and others. One person described it as hand to mouth living. Well, you rarely get quality nourishment from eating or living in that way. There is no time to defragment your hard disk. This is different from the creativity of making it up as you go along. Wandering aimlessly is actually part of the creative process, but gets missed if people are bound to the relentless pace.

You can't create if the pace is your priority. Speed of thinking and doing is not the same as forcing a pace. Speed is usually something that happens as a result of effective, appropriate and motivated (content) behaviour. Pace cannot force speed. Pace cannot force speed. Pace cannot force speed.

In rural Kentucky, an insurance salesman and a farmer are talking; as they speak, the phone rings. The farmer makes no move to answer it. The salesman asks him why he doesn't get the phone, and the farmer just shrugs his shoulders. The salesman asks him why he had it put in the first place, and the farmer replies that he had it put in for his own convenience. The farmer decided when he wanted to use the technology, not when he would be summoned by it.

It does not seem as though people want to address the impact pace has on their lives. They take up residence in the Denial Room under cover of project plans, serious, large, exhorting time planners and even more outrageous schedules. It all becomes something that is created "out there" rather than in their heads.

Several people have explained their actions by stating that everything you do in E companies you do by being fast, and that you only get momentum that way. Once you fail you can't get back on. In this hothouse environment, people become very focused on themselves, even when they are saying "Together we can win, but on our own we lose." Scratch the surface of statements like this, or ask people why a grillion awaydays with the team have made no difference to the relationships between them, and you find an incredible fear of personal failure.

What a sad indictment that people have so many stories to tell and no time to tell them; or feel they have no people to tell them to... *What kind of empty success do you create when the Pace is all you know?* People still want to work around people they like; for bosses they respect. None of that need has changed.

The person in charge of new Netscape open source projects is known as the Chief Lizard Wrangler. When she was asked what the difference between a manager and a wrangler was, she said she had to coordinate people she had no authority or line responsibility for. The name was used to signify a new way of working. (Notice they still use the word Chief......)

One person working in a cutting-edge E company described it in this way: "One thing that has really thrown me is the lack of hierarchy and the established 'crutch' of having a higher authority to appeal to for decisions (plus a lack of regular meetings – or in fact anything resembling a formal process of appraising what's happening). In my past lives, if I wanted to effect a change or do something which was potentially controversial, I would get buy-in from someone high enough to be able to force other people to co-operate (as it were). In this new world, this does not exist. For example, if I thought that it would be a great idea if everyone who worked within my company should use a certain supplier – even if there was a really good reason for doing so, nobody here would see it as their job to make that happen. Instead you have to rely on your powers of persuasion and reason to speak to people individually and be flexible enough to accommodate people who don't see it in the same way as you might. Most of the discussions I have had which were of any merit were walking to a sandwich shop with someone or standing outside having a cigarette. This is really weird but actually quite invigorating. Because if you achieve anything, it is down to merit rather than dictate. Instead of convincing maybe one or two people, you have to convince everyone. You have to be friends with everyone and you have to get to find out about what everyone does."

"IT'S NO LONGER ABOUT THE BIG BEATING THE SMALL, IT'S ABOUT THE FAST BEATING THE SLOW."
[LARRY CARTER, CFO OF CISCO SYSTEMS]

The pace winds itself up and up on a seemingly endlessly torquable ratchet. Is there a break point? There certainly is for humans; however cool and fast the technology, we have certainly not evolved as fast; that means our minds and emotions are playing catch-up with something that is taking us on a wild ride. Individuals have different break points; *will E commerce itself have one, probably driven by the human element?* Very few people in the E world are prepared to countenance that right now, and those outsiders who fire shots across their bows get dismissed with accusation of "just jealous", "you just don't get it"..... When children get very hyped up and overexcited, parents frequently say, "This will end in tears." *Is this a scenario for the hyperkinetic E pioneers?* Examine your pace. Examine the pace of the people you work with. Examine how it affects your ability to work together, both positively and negatively.

E-world pace is controlled by the people in it, not the technology.

"OF COURSE IT'S INSANE...
THAT'S WHY IT'S THE ONLY THING TO DO."

[SPACE]
AND RELATIONSHIPS

"THE SPACE BETWEEN PEOPLE WORKING TOGETHER IS FILLED WITH CONFLICT, FRICTION, STRIFE, EXHILARATION, DELIGHT AND VAST CREATIVE POTENTIAL. ALLOW SPACE FOR THE IDEAS YOU HAVEN'T HAD YET AND THE IDEAS OF OTHERS."

[*ID* MAGAZINE]

"WITHIN THESE PLACES, SOCIAL CONTACTS WILL BE MADE, ECONOMIC TRANSACTIONS WILL BE CARRIED OUT, CULTURAL LIFE WILL UNFOLD, SURVEILLANCE WILL BE ENACTED, AND POWER WILL BE EXERTED."

[WILLIAM MITCHELL]

"LIFE IS A

BIFURCATING CHAOTIC ATTRACTOR,

AND THEN
YOU DIE."

[R.U. SIRIUS]

SPACE – THE FINAL FRONTIER.....

We are told we live in a shrinking world, with Cyberspace as the seventh continent. Unfortunately, that way of thinking makes it another place as opposed to a place which underpins the vast majority of our activities to a greater or lesser extent.

When we think of space, we usually think of physical space and environment. This is a determining factor in relationships and the E world's environment, and where transactions, emotional and commercial, take place impacts not only the place, but the type of transaction. Physical space is not the only determinant of space; we need to consider psychological spaces that are created, and that we create and define for ourselves in this world. *What exactly is Cyberspace?*

William Gibson is credited with inventing the word in his novel *Neuromancer*, describing it with these phrases:

> "A CONSENSUAL HALLUCINATION EXPERIENCED DAILY BY BILLIONS OF LEGITIMATE OPERATORS, IN EVERY NATION......A GRAPHIC REPRESENTATION OF DATA ABSTRACTED FROM THE BANKS OF EVERY COMPUTER IN THE HUMAN SYSTEM. UNTHINKABLE COMPLEXITY. LINES OF LIGHT RANGED IN THE NONSPACE OF THE MIND, CLUSTERS AND CONSTELLATIONS OF DATA. LIKE CITY LIGHTS, RECEDING."

Got it? It's not really a place; it's places. It's not really a space; it's notional spaces. *What has its existence meant to finding "place" in the world? Are our relationships any different there than in the wired world? If so, what makes it so?*

In the words of a manifesto by MIT research scientist David Clark, "We reject: kings, presidents and voting. We believe in: rough consensus and running code." (Only the privileged few at that time understood the implications of this technology, of course.) According to these cyber-pioneers, Cyberspace could only be free; freedom was its nature. The word ironically does not speak of freedom, but control. Cybernetics is the study of control at a distance. The term was coined by Professor Norbert Weiner for his book of the same name in 1948. From the Greek for steersman, he defined it in a subtitle as "control and communication in the animal and the machine".

Many would say that E commerce is control at a distance. Much of the Internet anarchy which enabled it to develop also creates huge problems for those who wish to have more control. *Who, if anyone, really owns Cyberspace? Are we all responsible for it?*

Lawrence Lessig takes a detailed look at the macro responsibility issues, such as liberty, legislation and regulation, in his book *Code and Other Laws of Cyberspace*. It is a complex question. Both government and commerce are in a position to change what the Internet is. The "early adopters" still see it as "their space" and consider themselves "libertarians". Lessig makes the point that if there are founding values of the Net that are values worth defending, they are worth defending against any threat, commercial, governmental or individual.

In terms of how that affects you at work, it means that the things you do come back to haunt you much quicker and with more directness; you are responsible. In terms of managing self and others at work, that means a lot more care and attention in an environment which is not immediately obviously conducive to paying attention to others.

IT MEANS BEING MORE DIRECT, WHICH SAVES TIME.
IT MEANS LEARNING TO BE CLEAR ABOUT WHAT YOU WANT BEFORE YOU SAY ANYTHING.
IT MEANS UNDERSTANDING WHAT YOU NEED TO DO TO GET YOUR MESSAGE ACROSS.
IT MEANS BEING ABLE TO TALK IN CLEAR, PRECISE AND NON-JUDGMENTAL LANGUAGE.

"YOU SIMPLY MENTION A CHAIR

AND IT'S SHADOWY.

YOU SAY IT'S STAINED
WITH WEDDING SAFFRON

AND SUDDENLY

THE CHAIR IS THERE."

[KEN LOACH]

This ability to be clear in a fast space is crucial. We consciously or subconsciously define our space professionally and personally. *Are we defined by what we do rather than how we do it? Are there special "definers" for the E world?*

> "WE DON'T HAVE ROOTS. WE'RE NETWORK PEOPLE. WE HAVE AERIALS."
>
> [CHARACTER IN *DISTRACTION* BY BRUCE STERLING]

One of the key definers we use to both recognize and explain is language. If all we do is put our antennae up and don't transmit, we are unlikely to connect, just absorb. After a while people stop giving you data. The E world has developed its own language to cope with the speed of connection, and it can be very excluding... The language of the wired world is very specific and very definitive.

> "HE HAS NO RESET BUTTON"
> "JUST DOUBLE CLICK ON YOURSELF, AND YOU'RE THERE"
> "LISTENING TO HIM IS LIKE PRESSING THE SCAN BUTTON..."
> "SHE IS DEFINITELY SHORT ON PORTAL ACCESS."
>
> [OVERHEARD IN VARIOUS CONVERSATIONS]

What is scary is the number of people who knew exactly what the person meant by very clear technological descriptions. I'll bet you did. They have, in these cases, become shorthand for describing a phenomenon that everyone familiar with that world understands. Most people who relate to each other on a regular basis end up with some form of shorthand, both personal and professional. They use this to speed up communication; most times it becomes subconscious. The problems arise when someone enters the communication who is not steeped in that particular language. This becomes particularly acute in cross-functional teams, where finance people, technocrats and sales people expect one another to understand their shorthand. It happens when parents expect their children to understand their shorthand. Interestingly enough, teenagers have no expectation that their parents will understand them, in fact expect them not to. This is often played out with technogeeks who do not expect the world to understand them, and don't actually care whether the world does understand. Initially at Microsoft, Bill Gates seemed to understand this, and allowed them to talk among themselves and be sheltered from the rest of the company. However, if you don't keep an eye on the changing habits of a population, they end up surprising you. Even Microsoft now cannot get all the people it needs to staff its expansion. What the world needs now is more babel fish or at least universal translators...

> "... IF YOU STICK A BABEL FISH IN YOUR EAR YOU CAN INSTANTLY
> UNDERSTAND ANYTHING SAID TO YOU IN ANY FORM OF LANGUAGE."
>
> [DOUGLAS ADAMS, *THE HITCH HIKER'S GUIDE TO THE GALAXY*]

So, short of an invasion of babel fish, how can we seriously improve the way in which we define ourselves and our workspaces?

NEW CONDITIONS DEMAND A NEW WAY OF THINKING.
NEW WAYS OF THINKING DEMAND A NEW MODE OF EXPRESSION.
EXPRESSION GENERATES NEW CONDITIONS....

Many natural linguists will tell you that it isn't the words that enable you to speak a language; it's hearing the rhythms and flows. It's often helpful not to know the words so that you are more aware of the cultural non-verbals, or the tone in people's voices. Sometimes the words get in the way of any language. The E world is no exception. The language can sound unintelligible and daunting, but if you listen beyond that noise, it's the same stuff, just sung with different music. Anyone can hum that tune.

"IT ISN'T THE WORDS THAT MATTER, IT'S THE TUNE THAT TELLS THE STORY."
[CECIL SKLAN]

WHAT IS THE RHYTHM OF THE E-WORLD SPACE?
Sometimes the only tune you can hear is Pace, Pace, Pace. No Space. At this point it becomes less of a tune, and more of a relentless, pounding technobeat, which becomes almost hypnotic. *What helps us define, and what gets in the way?* In this wired and uncertain world, people often look for definition where there is none. *Why do we still want it? Why isn't there any?*

The usual response is that speed has become the driver and therefore definition goes out of the window. *Why should that happen?* It doesn't seem as though it is the speed itself that is doing the driving. It is the people operating at speed that are forcing the pace and losing their definition. *So why do we allow that to happen?* Ask anyone in today's world whether they have enough time and most people will answer in the negative. Some will say "Enough to do what? To be what?" Therein lies the rub. *Why do people in Silicon Valley work a minimum of seven days a week to unachievable deadlines?* Some will say that it's the money; others a desire to achieve, others because that's the way it is. *Have they defined it, or allowed it to define them?* Larry Ellison and Bill Gates would never ever have to work again if they stopped now, and yet they have no desire to. *When the young Silicon Valley entrepreneurs make their first million, how many of them actually stop?* There is as yet very little hard data, but it's certainly an unusual event to hear of these guys heading for the hills or the beach for permanent residence. *What defines You and your relationships in the E world? Whilst the E world does have a language of its own which is easy to pick up, how do You personally connect? How distant are You from the way you feel others behave in the workplace? What would You need to do to have a tighter connection?*

RANDOMNESS OF RELATIONSHIPS

One of the delights and inspirations of living life is absorbing its random nature, and creating space in your life for it to happen. No time means no time for the serendipity of a meeting in a coffeehouse, or idle banter. Even the coffeehouse meetings are under a time pressure, or for a purpose. The coffeehouses have never been more plentiful, or more full. Listen to the conversations. *What happened to chat? The lightness of being and having fun with others?*

The fun seems to come from work-related issues or very hard play; but not from chance encounters or light moments. Even in many organizations where they have constructed "coffeehouse environments", what gets discussed are deadlines, not ideas or working relationships. *What kind of space do we take nowadays to share with others?*

One artist tells of how he drives a San Francisco cab to make money, and finds that people either say nothing to him, or they spill out their life story. The latter only happens when he asks them questions about themselves. (He figured that he knew what he had to say and other people were way more interesting...) *What does this tell us about the way we relate in the wired world?*

It seems as though we get into a taxicab, and we are in transition from one space to another; this limbo either makes us clam up as we are not in a known space, or makes us feel we are in undefined, unowned space which will never come again; therefore it's safe to speak. In the fast lane where every second has to be used, the neutral zone of the taxi is used as a dumping ground. *Is this a relationship?* Well in the purest sense, it's two people interacting, but whether it moves from being from a conversation to a relationship is debatable.

People talk about what they want to do and how they want to do it....actually, it may be the only space they have. It may also be that by E-world standards, any conversation doth a relationship make. *Does the pace of the techno-environment make your work relationships only functional and totally related to the job in hand? Just the contrast with walking and talking – where did you go to talk? Why there? Is there something about the relationship to movement and thought and the consequent conversation that you lose sitting behind a computer screen? Does this "office/techno-environment" contribute in part to sustaining a functional flavour, in both the language we use and the subjects we communicate about?*

It's hard to recall "remember when" conversations that have happened on email. They seem to be fixed in a moment in time and not necessarily meant to recall that moment. That is very different to recalling both a conversation and the environment in which it occurred. Frequently, the environment has contributed to the nature and course of the interaction. It's hard to do that when you are talking on your cell phone, whilst driving. This does not build relationships, or give them anything to progress to. All conversations therefore begin to centre around a specific objective. Pretty soon, that way of speaking has translated itself to every walk of your life, so that your children have to fix appointments with you, or get your voicemail.

Even as I was writing this I was reminded of a conversation I had with a friend while walking in the fields above my house. This conversation was nine years ago, but I can remember what we said, and can picture both people. If I contrast that with a conversation I had with the same person two weeks ago, it was about no less important a subject, but it was started on email and finished on the telephone, and my memory of it has no anchors. I can remember the outcome, but nothing about how we got there, or what either myself or the other person was thinking or feeling. This has huge implications for the development of all relationships, and also on the kind of environments that encourage learning. *If learning is dependent on enquiry, dialogue, assumption testing and explorations, what happens if those conditions are not present? Does this suggest email supports brilliant exchanges of info and even ideas, but slows or changes a lasting learning process?* This is exactly the kind of discussion that needs to be walked and talked, not didactically imparted in a book, or gleaned off a website.

Some things need "connected" space, not isolation. Some don't. Defining space is about working out what is important for that particular situation. If things are not working as effectively as they might be, try changing the environment or space.... (after all, that is part of what we do when we take a holiday).

This is an extract from an email sent to me by a colleague with some thoughts he had about the subject of the book. He basically used the space on the screen to dump his thoughts. Whilst I know what he was trying to say (I think), if I wanted to enrich and develop the discussion, I would want to do as he said and walk and talk it. The "I think" in brackets is often where our inferences take us. We think we know what others are thinking, but we are not in their thinking space. If their moment in time is different to ours, we have both taken different roads.

"Post-structuralist view would be that once written words have their own physical existence (autoglotic space I think it's called?) which adds a dimension to the interpretive process. (perhaps this would aid inquiry? an email exchange would be easier to analyse a la Argyris / 2 columns?) Wonder if we mentally map our email contacts/recipients still on a geographical basis? Visualise the office/home they receive in? We struggle with 'nowhere' and replace by somewhere when we can. How do we work on 'process' with email relationships? Perhaps illustrates the possibilities but issues – I'd like to talk and walk this one!"

So the space we use, live in and need: Has E living changed it? Does the E world change our perceptions and need for space/"home"?

HOME IS WHERE THE CONNECTION IS

Our home roots, where we have our personal safe haven, are very important to our ability to operate effectively in the workplace. *Has the E world changed any of that?* The blurring of boundaries between home and work means that the home, or home workplace needs have changed. There is a huge body of written data of a demography that is changing with and as a result of new technology. It is hard to know whether it is just the E world or people. *So what changes in people's need for "home" have been observed?* Opinion polls have long suggested a preference among a significant proportion of both Americans and Europeans to reside in smaller places. Many people still retain a strong attachment to the rural ideal. (Witness the growth and membership of the Countryside Alliance in the UK.) The draw of non-metropolitan areas stems not only from the desire to retreat from the big city stresses and hazards, but also from the desire to live in a community where people know one another, where they can make a difference, and live in closer touch with nature. There is a difference between being in a rural area and being of it...... It is hardly surprising that people want to live in pretty places. What is interesting is the extent to which scenic beauty is becoming a major factor in their life decisions, among all class and income levels. Poverty with a view.

One story of a thirtysomething who moved from Silicon Valley to the mountains of the Pacific NorthWest. When she first arrived, she was stunned by Woody Guthrie's "endless skyway" and green forests. She was anxious to get away from her three-hour commute and relentless work pressure. Be careful what you wish for.......she got her wish, at half her original salary, at a secretarial job. But she does get to ride her bike every night for two hours. Many people have the same ambivalence; it may well be that if technology can reach the far-flung places, many can still have the lifestyle they aspire to, in the place they want to be in. Right now it is not available.

Some argue that as more people work from home, they look for more communal activity in their neighbourhood, and therefore encourage the growth of neighbourhood services like coffeehouses, health clubs etc. People are often around during the day; the 9 – 5 way of being is eroded by homeworking. Starbucks have taken over many old banks that have been replaced by online banking.

"WHO LIVES HORIZONTALLY
IS NEVER SOMEWHERE,
BUT ALWAYS IN PASSAGE."

[JAMES CARSE]

So, does the wired world foster disconnection? Or do people do it? Given the increasing trend towards individual goods and services, privatized, individualistic solutions, how does this affect social cohesiveness and the way we live?

For most of our life as a species, many goods were shared. Private property made little sense to nomads or itinerant workers. However, tribal societies were very touchy on the subject of territory and natural resources; they were often seen as the binding force for a community. Indeed, they were frequently used as a call to arms – and still are.

In the 1950s, sociologist David Reisman wrote that we are a "lonely crowd", living and working within feet of people whose names we will never know. When you talk to people in the cities today, they all bemoan this and speak of wanting to be in a friendly neighbourhood. They do not want to give up any of their privacy to get this...

Joel Garreau, in his book *Edge Cities*, suggests that the money is in places called Edge Cities. They are a transportation nexus for cars and planes, and now the Infobahn. They are usually situated at major road intersections, and are often the first places to receive the fibre-optic cable infrastructure being put in by telephone companies. He suggests that there are 181 Edge Cities in America, each of which is larger than Memphis, e.g. Denver. He suggests these as the communities for Cyberspace:

"I DISAGREE WITH THE LINE WHICH HOLDS THAT CYBERSPACE DOOMS CITIES FOREVER, THAT IF YOU HAVE ENOUGH BANDWIDTH YOU CAN LOCATE ON YOUR OWN MOUNTAINTOP IN MONTANA AND BE LURED INTO THE FLATLANDS ONLY TO BREED. THAT IS A PROFOUND MISREADING OF HOW HUMANS WORK. WE ARE SOCIAL BEINGS."

"**FACE TO FACE CONTACT** WILL BE
THE ONE AND ONLY POINT OF CITIES
IN THE FUTURE. WE HAVE BEEN TELLING
EACH OTHER STORIES AROUND THE
CAMPFIRE FOR MILLENNIA AND A LITTLE
SILICON CHIP IS NOT GOING TO CHANGE
THAT. THE WINNING EDGE CITIES ARE
GOING TO BE THE OBVIOUS PLACE
TO GO FOR THAT **FACE TO FACE CONTACT.**"

[JOEL GARREAU]

Michael Porter, in his studies of economic geography, describes the ascendancy of a "city-state". Silicon Valley is a city state, running from San Francisco to San José. These clusters of "exuberant variety" are at the heart of entrepreneurship and progress. *But what is it that makes it so? Could it have anything to do with the fact that an awful lot of like-minded people are gathered in the same location, and understand each other? Something to do with relationships?*

Some futurologists paint a very cosy picture of how technology will "glue the family unit back together again". One sees technology as a way of families working together as a unit, and is thinking about a return to living above the shop, the weaving loom in the living room and the farmhouse dairy. However, to another, this looks like an attempt to imprison people in what was their "safe haven". It can take away any refuge from the workplace, encourages long and irregular hours, and eliminates any sense of perspective about the different facets of our lives and their relative importance.

The question as ever comes down to one of balance. How can we balance this potential equalizing mechanism, which can greatly enhance the lives of the housebound and isolated, and those who are vehicularly challenged, with its potential to imprison and create even more isolation. William Mitchell, in his book *City of Bits*, discusses how we are defined by our spaces; going to work, going out, going to college and coming home are all significant socially and legally defining acts. To change or eliminate them, may be to fundamentally alter the basic fabric of our everyday lives.

He makes the distinction between the two Latin words *civitas* and *urbs*: "Families or tribes who joined together because they shared the same religious beliefs, social organisation, form of government and modes of production created 'civitas' – a community that was not necessarily related to any particular place or construction. But when such a unity chose a particular site and founded a city in which to dwell – as Rome was founded on seven hills – an 'urban' settlement resulted. So urban space became the territory of the civic formation, and civic principles determined the spatial configuration of the city. Choice of site, performance of the foundation ritual and organisation of the layout were seen as such fundamentally important acts that they were traditionally ascribed to the community's gods and mythic heroes." (Maybe the building of the new Science and Technology Park in Cambridge will reflect the mythic status of its benefactor, William Gates.)

Whilst this phenomenon is more marked in the US, possibly due to the distance between most cities and easy rural access, as a converse proposition, the Europeans seem to be drifting "downtown"....

There are large numbers of people who see themselves as urban; they are equally at home in New York, London, Amsterdam or Prague, and often have an equal knowledge of the social environs of these cities.

The Net money has changed the face of places like San Francisco. It has driven up the price of a condo to $410,000; a rise of 40% in a year. Many of the middle class are moving out of the city to suburban areas they can afford, and the homeless population keeps on growing. Overcrowded transport and shopping areas, to say nothing of the permanent traffic congestion, add to people's frustration with the deteriorating quality of life in the city. The atmosphere has also changed from easygoing and tolerant to materially oriented, pushy and excluding.

You decide whether that is a space you want to inhabit, change or exit. As economist Robert Frank points out,

> "IN THE END, YOU END UP A MUCH MEANER SOCIETY. IT'S IRONICALLY A SOCIETY THAT PEOPLE AT THE TOP DON'T FIND ATTRACTIVE EITHER. THEY HAVE TO SIT IN THE SAME TRAFFIC JAMS AS US."

This same story is echoed in many places in Northern California. *Will it have a similar effect in Europe?* The concentration of E-commerce and high-tech organizations is nowhere near as great as in The Bay Area and Silicon Valley of Northern California. The need for space has always been reflected differently in Europe, in terms of respect for history and character of cities. Time may tell....

"**AMERICA** IS WHAT PEOPLE CREATED WHEN THEY WERE SICK TO DEATH OF EUROPE.
NORMALCY FOR AMERICA – IT ISN'T KEEPING YOUR NOSE CLEAN AND COUNTING YOUR CARBON DIOXIDE.
NORMALCY FOR AMERICA IS TECHNOLOGICAL CHANGE."

[CHARACTER IN *DISTRACTION*, BY BRUCE STERLING]

Is there a pattern or do we just want to see one and hold the E world responsible?

So, what kind of space do work "communities" need to function effectively in the E world?
The word "community" is used ad nauseam, but what does it mean in terms of customer and user?
Now, a community need not find its roots in a geographic place, but in cyberspace.
Most Internet companies will talk about the two "C" words all the time: Community
and Co-creation. People hear and mean different things....

Often a community reflects a space to be, and in that sense there are many successful
working communities in the E world. Some of them were created specifically, some
happened; but they share the fact that like any successful group, the members are clear
about what they want from the community.

One example of a working successful Internet community can be found in the Linux
story. Linux is a free version of the Unix operating system, and was written by Linus
Torvalds, a student at the University of Helsinki, with a legion of collaborators. From the
start, he made the source code available on the Internet. As users tinkered with it,
discovered bugs, and suggested fixes, a global virtual community of Linux developers
sprang up. Today Linux runs on one sixth of business server computers and is growing...

Torvalds and his collaborators had set out to show that they could build a better system
for free than Microsoft or IBM could do with their billions. Some observers attribute
their success to the Internet's ability to nurture fluid working communities. Eric
Raymond, in his book *The Cathedral and the Bazaar*, believes that their success was down
to turning the traditional software development model, which was based on hierarchy,
central control and secrecy, on its head. He writes, "I believed that the most important
software needed to be built like cathedrals, carefully crafted by individual wizards or
small bands of mages working in splendid isolation, with not a beta release before its
time." As a complete contrast, the Linux community resembled "a great babbling
bazaar of differing agendas and approaches". His conclusions were, "Release early.
Release often. And listen to your customers."

Open source faith had been at the heart of the development of Internet infrastructure,
with TCP/IP the Internet's standard transmission protocol; SMTP for email; and
Apache the software that powers more than 60% of Web servers. Raymond says that for
hackers, building systems that benefit all is a form of play and partly a matter of
prestige. Programmers volunteer to tackle complex problems because it's exciting to
find a solution, and when you can turn that solution over to the community, that feels
even better, as it reflects well on the giver.

This is an interesting culture of people who come together as a community in Cyberspace knowing that there is no leader to hold them together, and no one person's idea is more or less likely to be accepted. There is no right or wrong way to do things, and no punishment. This community would be unlikely to achieve what they have if those basic fundamentals changed.

For some people a "community" is a collection of consumers, with similar needs. For others it is still a group of people who interact and respond to each other's needs. Many will argue that that exactly describes an effective provider/customer relationship; the difference is in what is provided by the interactive relationship. Tangible results which involve economic transactions are more likely to be customer-based and dependent on supply and demand. Interactions which involve less tangible results, such as learning, awareness and reciprocity, are more likely to be "community"-oriented in the true sense of the word. Most commercial online ventures earn money by charging access or subscription fees, selling advertising or selling goods. Some of the smaller, original systems, like the Well, belong to the more communitarian tradition. They exchange information based on a shared commitment to the common good.

It does seem as though many producers know that the latter is what people really seek, and use the tangible benefits of consumption to appear to meet that need. The culture of open source and its communities bears no resemblance to what the large corporations and sales people talk about when they use the word community. There are also many products that have grown through the Net that show how shared values and an unimpeded culture can create responsive communication. People of like interests, sharing information, constitute the very history of the Internet. The scientists, who initially dominated usenet, posting news of their discoveries and discussing their implications in newsgroups, were the first open source journalists.

Slashdot.com is a dedicated community that acts as a clearing house and event space for computer news. Almost a "best of" the Web. Unlike big business press, which relies on journalists serving as gatekeepers who decide what deserves to be called news, Slashdot regulars are providers of news as well as consumers. This also makes the process of information collection inexpensive. Of course filtering out harmful or just plain wrong information remains the main hazard for open source journalism for practitioners as well as readers. You could argue that that is true of all media.....

The message in this case is "caveat emptor". You get greater speed, diversity and detail, but you sacrifice standards of fairness, objectivity and accuracy that ostensibly guide the "professional" media. Rob Malda, the man who started Slashdot, says that "We take the responsibility of the fact-checking department and put it into the hands of our readers." That is a fundamental difference between how traditional press and open source journalism sites relate to their audiences. Mainstream media expect readers to be passive, so that the fact it is written in the *Financial Times* is reason enough for readers to trust the news they consume. That kind of brand blind faith is often crucial to a company's marketing strategy.

In contrast, those who follow the Drudge report, usenet or Slashdot know that the information they are getting can't be accepted at face value. Readers are forced to rely on multiple sources before they accept a report as true. In short, they have to take responsibility for what they read. *I wonder if that is too much trouble for people in this speedy E age. Would you rather take your chances than take responsibility yourself? Will that ever get transferred to a broader populace?* If it does, it means that most corporate marketing plans would have to be reconsidered.

"In short, they have to take responsibility for what they read."

They have to take responsibility for their own spaces and what they put in them. It is this last point which is where the really interesting potential for the future development of relationships lies. It becomes your space. You create it and are responsible for it.

In this world, the responsibility for both seeking and verifying and even reporting information can be vested in the same person. It is their responsibility what they seek and write about and how they write it. This accountability is what attracts some and terrifies others. Sometimes it's great to have a scapegoat, someone to blame. Effective and productive relationships depend on the ability to take responsibility for your own thoughts and actions, whether you are choosing to stay in a relationship or choosing a website to visit.

This is a long way from the generally held view of corporations who transfer their business online. They seem to be good at transferring the same "we know what's good for you" behaviours to E commerce. It is difficult to know whether taking that stance will develop customer relationships of the kind they profess to want. *Do you want to live in this kind of space? Are you prepared for it?*

.

WORKING SPACES

So, returning to the workplace, how are some E companies managing these tensions? One example of an organization trying ways of creating effective work communities is an incubator company called Brainspark. They incubate startups and provide them with support, connections and information on their way to going public.

Brainspark operates on a type of come and go community; share, talk, exchange – but no real in-depth relationships are built or even, so it seems, required. The people who take to this environment have no expectations of deep relationships, but do have a need to connect with others. People are always clustering in groups or moving from desk to desk with bits of paper. Meetings that take place are short and happen wherever the people happen to be, on a desk, or on the floor if that is the only space. It is a club rather than an open plan office, where everyone has lots to talk about. Disagreements occur but they are usually kept short, because people want to get on to discovering new ways of doing. So you might see a guy setting up a dental information website, talking to someone else from a website about pets, or the CEO talking to investment bankers about the next round of funding. This would all be in the same room, at the same time.

This is a start-up organization, and they are already about to move to larger premises where people will be more spread out. *Will they suffer the same teething problems that any organization faces moving from a small to medium-sized organization? Will the technology make a difference? Will the fact that they are all very young and highly motivated make a difference? Will the new space make a difference?*

Ask them; email them at brainspark.com and find out.

Both their marketing director and their HR director (for want of a better phrase) were asked what they were good at and then asked to write the kind of job they would like to have and do. They recruit people first, then find places to put them. They are very clear about attracting ideas, and want to break away from the old school – people who want to get things done, but in a different way from the old hierarchical way. (When they worked out that the cream of software developers liked surfing and getting up late, they set up an office in Brighton; Brainspark by the sea...)

They all share an energy and dynamism to make it work. Most people who walk into their space say it feels like you are on holiday...i.e. everyone is enjoying themselves and doing what they want to do in order to get things done. Many have come there from large, often six-figure, salaries, to work for a tiny wage and equity and freedom. Because no one person's idea is better or worse than anyone else's, they have a much clearer professional respect for what people are really like, and what they can realistically achieve. *Will these kinds of companies become as inbred as large corporations and suffer the same consequences?*

It's hard to imagine too much innovation at companies where ninety per cent of the population are the same gender, about the same age, have a similar educational background, dress the same way and enjoy the same music. Lack of innovation is not necessarily a province of age. It happens to anyone who shuts themselves down to possibility and diversity of thought. If I substituted "all play golf" as the last descriptor, I could have been describing the last bastions of the male, western mega-corporation..... We seem to need identity, a tribe we feel we belong to, and sometimes that translates to a place that we feel comfortable in. If we feel too enmeshed in that place, we become dependent. A productive, growing community always needs new blood, and sometimes new space, to enrich itself.

We are a complex set of beings, feeling the need for safety and for stimulation.

FIGURES IN YOUR LANDSCAPE

Shifting gears a little, let's move from the physical space you seek to the ability to create what you seek in the workplace and in your personal life. *How does your ability to be innovative and creative help develop the environments that you want and need?* The future of your space lies in an ability to adapt and create. The space, pace, depth and timeframes of the E world are predicated on your being able to do things differently. *How do people create and re-create their space so that they can live in it successfully, happily and comfortably?*

".... IF YOU HAVE A PICTURE OF A LANDSCAPE, YOU LOOK AT IT AND YOUR EYE MOVES FREELY OVER THE LANDSCAPE; IF YOU PUT A HUMAN FIGURE IN THERE, EVEN IF IT'S A TINY LITTLE ONE, IT BECOMES THE CENTER OF YOUR ATTENTION. IT'S VERY DIFFICULT TO IGNORE, BECAUSE HUMANS RELATE TO OTHER HUMANS. WITH MUSIC IT BECAME A PROBLEM, BECAUSE I FELT THAT AS LONG AS I WAS IN THE CENTER OF THE PICTURE THIS KEPT YOU, AS THE LISTENER, OUTSIDE THE PICTURE. NOW IF I TOOK MYSELF OUT OF THAT PICTURE, THIS LEFT A KIND OF OPEN FIELD, A SOUND-FIELD OF SOME KIND, WHICH INVITED YOU IN; AND I FELT THAT BY REMOVING MY OWN PERSONALITY – AS REPRESENTED BY MY VOICE – I OPENED UP THE MUSIC IN A NEW WAY. I MADE A SPACE THAT PEOPLE COULD COME. JUST THAT SINGLE ACT MADE THE MUSIC MUCH MORE 'ENVIRONMENTAL'."

[BRIAN ENO]

There is a direct link here with leaders getting people to "buy in" to the vision they create. Instead of providing landscape, and encouraging people to paint themselves into the vision, many leaders simply drop their visions on to employees who have no real involvement, and therefore no commitment. It stays the leader's space as opposed to everyone's. In an E community it is often the issue that makes start-ups successes or failures. *How can you do this quickly and successfully in such a turbulent world?*

Innovation is one of the key buzzwords for success in the E world; it becomes a kind of Holy Grail, without much thought for creating spaces that support individuals and organizations in being innovative. There are probably two key ways to enable innovation: through a recipe or through artistry. A recipe is exactly what it sounds like: various ingredients put together under instruction and guidelines, which produce a known output. Artistry is about creating something new, with no pre-known result.

"ANY SUFFICIENTLY ADVANCED TECHNOLOGY IS INDISTINGUISHABLE FROM MAGIC."

[A.C. CLARKE]

A recipe is controlled, focused and structured. It is also only valid situationally, can be irrelevant and boring, and can disadvantage you if you are competing against people as opposed to things.

Artistry is original, inspired and unique. It is also risky and unpredictable and has turbulent features. Whilst the E world may invite artistry, it is essential not to underestimate the value of reliability and safety when considering the people who have to work in the environment.

When you are competing against absolutes, for example clear and finite goals, you may be better off using a recipe, as it is more controllable and measurable. When you don't know, and are shooting against a goal of being the "best" or first, you need to be different, and on the edge of the bell curve. The E world is about competing to be different.

"... 'WHICH PATH DO YOU INTEND TO TAKE, NELL?'
SAID THE CONSTABLE, SOUNDING VERY INTERESTED.
'CONFORMITY OR REBELLION?'
'NEITHER ONE. BOTH ARE SIMPLE-MINDED –
THEY ARE ONLY FOR PEOPLE WHO CANNOT COPE
WITH CONTRADICTION AND AMBIGUITY'."

[NEAL STEPHENSON, *THE DIAMOND AGE*]

Most innovation tends to get generated by three key instigators:

→ A PROBLEM THAT NEEDS TO BE SOLVED
→ A DESIRE FOR A NEW WAY, OR INSPIRATION
→ AN ACCIDENT

Therefore, in order to be innovative you have to:

→ SOLVE A PROBLEM
→ HAVE A VISION OR INSPIRATION
→ MAKE SOME MISTAKES

Hilary Austen suggests people don't need recipes to be innovative, but you do need process heuristics or frameworks to guide them. She proposes three stages to this process:

1 DECOMPOSING WHAT NEEDS TO BE DONE OR HAS BEEN DONE
2 WHEN YOU HAVE THESE COMPOSITE PARTS, EXPLORING WHAT PEOPLE WHO ARE ALREADY GOOD AT IT ARE DOING, AND INVESTIGATING HOW THEY DO IT
3 ONCE UNDERSTOOD, YOU NEED TO WORK OUT HOW TO PERSONALIZE WHAT NEEDS TO BE DONE SO IT BECOMES YOURS

At any stage in this process, you are subject to the artistic tension that creates "traps" that stop you taking risks or opportunities: for example, fear of failure, looking stupid, being wrong. Also when you try a new idea, it is unskilled by definition, therefore you are likely to think it stinks. Evaluation of newness is an unfair test, and creates another trap which prevents you taking risks.

One of the reasons "skunkworks" work in incubator organizations or in some companies is that there is no expectation of success in an established definition. Success is defined by level of creative spirit, new ideas and energy – with no judgement.

Techies know if something is well done if it is worth talking about over a pizza with fellow techies, not if it made money. Their excitement comes from the innovation and making it work. This creates a tension between innovation in the workplace and the need to deliver.

One example of an organization that has built its success around supporting this tension is Pixar, a Northern California-based movie company. The organization has existed for 15 years, and unusually for a Silicon Valley company, the founders are still there. In the software world, to be successful, you need a compelling idea that is new and different, and the ability to get it into space first.

In the film business, you need to find the idea, and you also need a story that is good enough to sustain four years' work. The product is the story, the innovation is in the way it is told. The storytelling is determined by what is totally possible, as far out as you think you can see and then a little further. When these people begin a project they know that the vehicle that they create and launch is not the one they will land in. They know that in fours years the technology will have taken it somewhere else; so they have to build that into their plans. They are looking at what would really excite a six year-old now, and what will do it in four years' time. *So what sort of people make up an organisation that has to operate in this way?*

Pixar look for four critical attributes in their artists:

Breadth They look for people who have a very wide sphere of interest, who will look wider than the obvious and beyond what any tool or skill presents. This demands a high level of natural curiosity.

Depth This broad level of knowledge and interest has to be sustained by a level of mastery in something. The artists that Pixar is looking for will be creating whole worlds from blank space. Every piece of spontaneity is something you create, whether you are an actor, a systems designer or an animator. This creativity comes from the breadth of knowledge and things observed either in inanimate objects or in people. Most traditional arts have at their centre this sort of observation. Artists of any kind tend to observe, rather than just see. Animation tends to exhaust your tank of observation, so you also need to be able to develop or do things that refill the tank.

The last two attributes, Communication and Collaboration, are more about how you go about doing what you do. The ability to collaborate with others is valued as highly as creative ability. It's hard to work with someone who walks on water, but who you can't eat lunch with. In this culture, the success of a project revolves around a person's full commitment to the whole work, not just an individual's contribution. They even go so far as to describe the best creative work as being that which makes your collaborators look good.

The movie business is built around people hired for expertise, who leave the project when their expertise is spent. Engineers and technical people operate within a similar culture, where being right is more important than anything else. If you are technically wrong, nothing ever gets over that. Keeping those high standards, which are also motivators, and not crushing innovation or ideas are crucial to the company's success. One way to create "acceptable failure" is the "dailies" ritual. Every day the artists at Pixar review their work. Criticism of unfinished work is expected, from a group of people as opposed to one person, and related to the work, not the person. Its focus is from the customer's (audience's) point of view. This encourages iterative refinement of a piece of work, and also can establish a "final" boundary. In this space, the organization's commitment is to keeping artists' passions alive, because unless that happens there will be no excitement for the customer.

IN PANIC
"A BRILLIANT MIND

Can a teacher teach innovation? Encourage yes, teach... probably not....innovation is a huge deal in business literature, but it involves risk...can you teach risk?

THING TO SEE."
IS A WONDERFUL

[RUDOLF STEINER]

"THE CREATIVE IS FOUND IN ANYONE WHO IS PREPARED FOR SURPRISE."
[JAMES CARSE]

Lives can be replicated by machines. People should pay attention to the artistic part of them; it is that that's non-replicable...don't be an algorithm – that can be repeated...

"THE MOST BEAUTIFUL THINGS ARE THOSE THAT MADNESS PROMPTS AND REASON WRITES."
[ANDRÉ GIDE]

Hilary Austen suggests that being truly innovative ends up on a delusional scale. If you are an innovation machine, then you are probably delusional, so you may never connect. If you are occasionally innovative, you need to listen and observe and not judge. You cannot become an artist by becoming skilled, but you can use any number of skills and techniques in artistic activity. You cannot go to school to become an artist, but you can go to school as an artist. *Can you make a choice about being delusional?* If you choose to do it, and those who truly are seem bound by some unspeakable force... those who go to the really risky places know they are going to get beaten up. For example, once Joan of Arc knows she is not really being spoken to by God, can she still do the things she needs to do, because in a "real" world, they make no sense and are outrageously risky and will visibly get you beaten up?

There are many courses in how to be an entrepreneur. It is questionable whether you can teach someone to be an entrepreneur. You can teach them to run the restaurant, but you can't teach them to have the idea or take the risk. In summary, you can teach the "how to", but you can't teach them the content or the spark.

Is what we see in the E generation choiceful irrationality? Are they really taking risks? Are they deluded? Is it only the investment bankers who are choiceful? Certainly the money persons are not deluded; they take on long bets and draw on inside straights. *Is it just the volume that makes them the money?* You could also argue that most Internet start-ups today are built on a blend of incremental innovations in software and the pursuit of some market niche. If one venture fails, it is easy to move on to the next, refining the software a bit and going after a different market. This is not visionary risk-taking or innovation. You could argue that the guys with the really original ideas are deluded, and that's what makes it so hard for them to run the companies they start. Their motivation is to realise the dream, not dream it every night. There do not appear to be easy answers to these questions. We are in the middle of the experiment, and there has never been an experiment like this. We may never know how we have done until we look back, and by that time the E world will have moved on.

Chris Argyris suggests that the more data you have about your environment, the more "choiceful" you can be. Jim March suggests that it doesn't matter how much data you have: risk will always be a determining and unpredictable variable of any "choice". *If you know how your environment works, does it make it easier or more scary?* We can't know absolutely. Live it and find out. Forget technology and think with your mind. Creativity is not device-dependent.

To manage space in the E world, you need to personalize the recipes that work for you, take the risks on things that don't, and create a space where you:

"**HARVEST**
THE UPSIDE OF RECIPES
AND MANAGE
THE TURBULENCE
OF ARTISTRY."

[HILARY AUSTEN]

[TIME]
AND RELATIONSHIPS

REAL AND FAKE TIME

SPIRIT OF CONNECTION

THE END OR THE JOURNEY?

THE CHANGING ROOMS

PRICE OF TIME

STEALIN' TIME

SEVEN AGES OF MAN

TIME OF YOUR LIFE

THINKING BEYOND THE WAVE

"TIME PRESENT AND TIME PAST
ARE BOTH PRESENT IN TIME FUTURE,
AND TIME FUTURE CONTAINED IN THE PAST.
IF ALL TIME IS ETERNALLY PRESENT
ALL TIME IS UNREDEEMABLE."

[T.S. ELIOT]

"LET ME FORGET ABOUT TODAY UNTIL TOMORROW."

[BOB DYLAN]

CATCH A MEMBER OF THE E GENERATION SAYING THAT! I DON'T THINK SO...

Time. The one thing you can't buy; *or can you?* It certainly is every bit as valuable as money for the inhabitants of the E world. And yet, there is very little respect for either your own time or other people's.

We are so ambivalent about time. We want to have lots of it, yet when we find ourselves with it, we fill the time, not necessarily with what we want. *Do we actually want time? Or do we want time to do things?* If the latter is the case, then we need to decide what things we want to do, or accept what serendipity provides. Most of the time, we don't know what we want and just go with what gets given. We even hide behind that as a way of avoiding responsibility... "sorry don't have any time"... "no that would take too long"... "not now"... "I'll fit you in"... *How many of our most often used phrases revolve around time?* It does take time to do things now. *What is time for you and how does your attitude to it affect relationships?*

What governs your perception of time? This is not about speed or pace; it is about the way we perceive time; how we use it and what we value. It explores times in our lives, and the impact that the E world and others have on them.

REAL AND FAKE TIME

Life for many people seems to have become a perpetual transition without a visible resting point...There is no sense of time. People talk about real time, without talking about fake time. We talk about past, present and future. *Where is the present?* Just a fraction of a second before the supposed present moment lies the past; just a fraction of a second after it lies the future. As soon as we have spoken the word "now" it is in the past. Whilst we live in the present, it only comes into being in dependence on the past and future. Understanding this dependence on other things or persons is key to getting balance in the E world. There is no future without a present; what creates our present is the interlinking of relationships and events. One of the skills you lose when you lose your perspective on time is the ability to see connections between people, actions, words and thoughts. This isn't about speed of thought; it's about where you turn your thoughts.

There are times when you don't know who or what you want to do, be or say. Times when you don't know what kind of energy you have, don't have, or need. Times when you wonder who or what is really important. Those moments in time are usually inspired by events, usually dramatic ones that make you stop and think. *Do you know how to stop and think?*

Has living in the E world robbed you of that skill? Rob it right back. You need it to live healthily in any world. When you lose the ability to decide what you spend your time doing, you lose your identity.

Dramatic stuff; but seeing as how I am writing in the E world, I need to make dramatic statements even to touch you. *How do you get to rob your time back?* Well it isn't through paying someone to do your dry cleaning for you. That's just tinkering with the symptoms, like taking Night Nurse to "cure" a cold.

What is the cause of your time theft? How did it happen to you? What was it you were looking for when you gave it away? Did you find it?

SPIRIT OF CONNECTION

In the virtual world, no one cares whether you scream... well, they might if you took the time to invest in a relationship.

The spirit of connection. That is something you can't buy. Not even online. The desire for connection is part of the desire for community. The human need to be acknowledged, received and heard. For many, this came from the various communities people belonged to. *Have people lost the desire for community as we knew it? Have they actually increased desire?*

What seems to happen is people talk about it more, but actually don't want it. It takes too much time. In a similar way, kids talk about low self-esteem way more than they used to. However, the way they describe it sounds like a disease: "She has contracted low self-esteem." They know the words, but have no better an understanding of what it is or means. Listening to people talk about community, it feels the same way. They talk about community, trust, respect and belonging, but appear to have no conception of what that would look like, what they themselves would be doing if they were behaving in that way. Trust is not something you get by just asking for it.

So in this brave new E world how do people get along? What do they say and not say? What are the needs of the individual within it? The Dalai Lama has suggested that the millennium should be a time for dialogue; *do we know how to do that? Do we want it? Do we know what to say? Have we lost some of the desire for dialogue?* It doesn't seem to fit into our time schedules, and unless it seems to produce some kind of result, we seem to avoid putting aside time; in fact we usually say we have none to put aside. If no time is put aside, you can never develop interest, curiosity or enjoyment.

This is not about pace and speed; they are variables of time. This is about how we ascribe importance to situations and people. Time is about relationships: who, when, how much. Time is genetic – what you create today is your future. Unfortunately, the pace of the E world seems to create a sense of time which only relates to the present. Some will argue that that has a great deal to do with the major drivers of the E world, that is people aged between 17 and 35. Those people, in the natural cycle of human development, are in their most pushy phase because that is what their bodies and minds want them to do. Technology just fuels that furnace. It does decrease the possibility of relationships developing. All relationships need attention and time.....

"WITHOUT MEMORY OR HISTORY, INNOVATION IS ONLY NOVELTY. A MEMORY IS NEVER PERFECT AND IS SHROUDED IN THE MOMENT. ITS QUALITY LIES IN THE PAST – NOT ITS PRESENT. EVERY MEMORY IS NEW, A PARTIAL CONSTRUCT DIFFERENT FROM ITS SOURCE; AND AS SUCH A POTENTIAL FOR GROWTH IN ITSELF."

[*ID* ARTICLE]

THE END OR THE JOURNEY?

So where does our time context come from? Much of it comes not from our arrival, but from our journey to get there. In the E world, so much is focused on the end result that there is no importance placed on how you got there. You only live for the result. In the E world, getting the result means move to the next, as that is the only means of being validated or measuring achievement. The end. *What journey?*

> "IT'S TIME TO GET REAL. INTERNET ENTREPRENEURSHIP IS CHALLENGING, EXCITING AND POTENTIALLY LUCRATIVE. IT'S WORTH A TRY. STATISTICALLY, HOWEVER, BEING AN INTERNET ENTREPRENEUR IS THE EQUIVALENT OF SPINNING THE BIG WHEEL. ENTER THE CASINO WITH YOUR EYES WIDE OPEN. REMEMBER: THE JOURNEY IS YOUR REWARD."
>
> [BOB JACOBSON, SILICON VALLEY ASSOCIATION OF SOFTWARE ENTREPRENEURS]

How many of these guys believe that the journey is their reward? That's hard to believe on an 80-hour week with no time for anything....that is one hell of a journey....and if there is no time on the journey to watch and look around you, that sounds more like a business trip than a journey. Journey implies discovery.

There is a great deal of self-deception involved in our attitude to time. Self-deception/delusion is something we all do; sometimes in denial of what is happening or might happen; sometimes in protection, sometimes because it is a much more attractive picture. *At what point in time do we actually deal with the fact that we feel one thing and do another?* Perhaps it is not about deceit, but more about the loss of freedom that happens when we behave in this way. We often convince ourselves that we believe what we are doing or thinking, just as an actor convinces themselves that they are the part they are playing. *Can we ever totally conceal the delusion? How far will we go, and in terms of relationships, how far will we go to have others act complicitly with us?*

THE CHANGING ROOMS

The human mind is ingenious. When faced with a major change to a concept in reality, it will resort to any means or devices necessary to thwart that change. It will do anything to protect the old beliefs. Sometimes if you don't want to let go of a belief that something won't work, you create a long list of reasons for it not to. Some of our instincts and habits corrupt information we try and process; e.g. you feel you absolutely must reach a conclusion.

Ideas about Change are everywhere in our world. The Changing rooms are a way of expressing respected, conventional, collective wisdom. Everything that happens in our world is predicated on a change. We talk about change, sometimes without appreciating exactly what our minds need to go through to accept and make the change. We just want to be able to do it. Not only do we expect ourselves to do this, we expect others to. Mistake. We have to pass through various changing rooms before we move on to the next thing. For most people, when change affects you, it affects the relationships you have both at work and out of work.

Every change or difference in our lives means a loss. That is, a loss of what has been. The loss might be as trivial as changing the furniture in a room, or as serious as redundancy, but a loss is what it is. In the E world, these losses come so fast and furious that we don't even notice them; or at least we think we haven't, but some part of our heads has noticed that something has gone, and will be busy reacting to that. It is perfectly possible to be in several rooms at once.

"A THREAT OF LOSS CREATES ANXIETY, AND ACTUAL LOSS, SORROW;
BOTH, MOREOVER, ARE LIKELY TO AROUSE ANGER."

[JOHN BOWLBY]

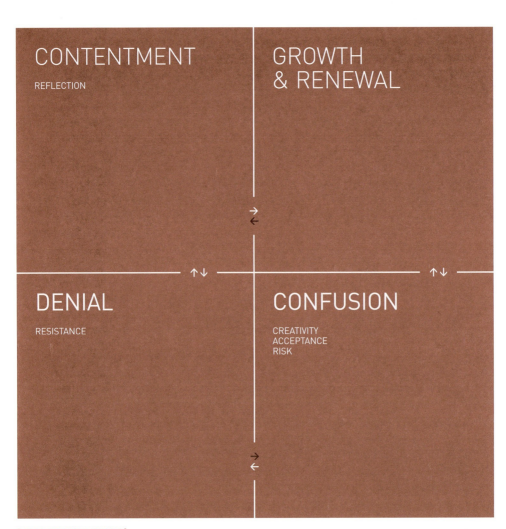

CONTENTMENT

REFLECTION

GROWTH
& RENEWAL

DENIAL

RESISTANCE

CONFUSION

CREATIVITY
ACCEPTANCE
RISK

[ADAPTED FROM JENSEN]

It is easier to picture the process of change by visualizing it as a four-room apartment. You can then see yourself and others in a "location". Being able to "see" psychologically helps to see yourself and others in reality.

The apartment consists of four rooms, which we will inhabit or pass through at some point during the change process. Each room represents a particular stage of the cycle. When we are familiar with people and situations in our lives, we are sitting in the Contentment room. In this room, we know exactly what the furniture looks like, we have chosen the wallpaper and the light fittings, we have our favourite comfy chair. The fire is lit, we have a warm cup of tea in our hands, and everything is cosy and safe. Sometimes we don't even know we are in the room, until we have been pushed out of it by changing circumstances. Other times we don't appreciate the time for rest, reflection and recovery that this room can provide after the traumas of Confusion and Renewal. Sometimes we can control our time in this room, other times not. Perhaps the more familiar we are with the process of change, the more we can appreciate the space in the Contentment room.

This is a room that most E workers would not be familiar with. It is a room where time is valuable for reflection, as opposed to action. It is not long, however, before change comes along and moves us into the next room. Once we are in there, there is no way back into the particular Contentment room we have just come from. The next time we see a Contentment room, it may look very different; indeed, we will make it so as a result of our experiences, but the principal dynamic of the room will remain the same. It does not matter how familiar you are with those processes, it doesn't stop you from going through them. Being aware of them, however, will enable you to accept and deal with them and move on. There is nothing that can take away the pain, anxiety and confusion of loss. Don't try to! The cycle needs to be gone through.

Once evicted (or even voluntarily ejected) from the Contentment room into the Denial room, every bone in our body tries to scream that nothing has changed, that everything is still the same. This prevents us having to deal with the pain of the loss. If we can pretend nothing has happened, we don't have to change anything in our lives. Denial has become one of those words in the E world that is bandied about, like community.... *If you have to talk about it or accuse someone of it, where are you? So why is the Denial room so attractive?*

Some of the attraction has to do with our personal picture of ourselves; the self concept. This is the essence and soul of ourselves and we therefore quite rightly guard it closely and jealously. It's the soft squidgy bit inside of us that we don't like anyone coming near, and do anything we can to preserve. For this reason we find some things extremely easy to talk about, that is those things that don't come anywhere near the squidgy bit. For example, talking about the weather, sport, other people, the theatre is easy. However, switch the conversation to feelings, hopes, fears, success and failure and watch it dry up.

SELF CONCEPT

THE SOFT SQUIDGY BIT ↗

Whenever conversation starts around these kinds of subjects, the soft squidgy bit goes into protection mode. It avoids any contact by use of defence mechanisms. These come in many different guises:

TALK ABOUT SOMEONE ELSE
CHANGE THE SUBJECT
DENY
LIE
PRETEND TO MISUNDERSTAND
GO QUIET
SHOUT
DISCOUNT
BLAME SOMEONE ELSE
BLAME THE SPEED OF LIFE
APPEAR TO CONFORM OR CONFESS TOO QUICKLY
MAKE A JOKE
YES, BUT
BURY YOURSELF IN TIME SCHEDULES
I DIDN'T MEAN TO....

the list goes on and on... one interesting exercise is to compile your own defence mechanisms.

Some of the defence mechanisms are our way of coping, the only way we can handle a loss. For example, with a loss of a partner, some people pretend the person is still there, and keep their clothes in a wardrobe, waiting for them to come back. Intellectually they know a loved one has died, but emotionally the loss is too hard to acknowledge. Sometimes this way of coping is appropriate to allow breathing space. This is very different to denying an event. They are after all protecting our soft squidgy bit.....
When a coping mechanism becomes a way of being, you have taken up residence in the Denial room.

The defence mechanisms share a common trait: they all avoid the individual taking responsibility for their own actions. If they don't own up to an action then there is nothing to change...

Another feature of the Denial room is that from its vantage point, we can see through the doorway into the Confusion room. And that is exactly what it looks like: fog, confusion. Sometimes we will take one step into the Confusion room and feel so mixed up that we move immediately back into the Denial room, for perceived safety. *What is it we are so scared of?*

Most of the time it is the unknown that we fear most; the unfamiliar. That fear will never be disposed of. We need to be able to acknowledge it, not hide from it. Sometimes denial gets us into some pretty sophisticated patterns of behaviour; even when you understand the process, it is easy to get caught up in the complexity of denial. Gestalt theorists describe this behaviour as resistance:

WHERE THERE IS A DRIVING FORCE FOR CHANGE,
THERE EXISTS A COMPLEMENTARY FORCE AGAINST IT.
RESISTANCE IS NOT AN ABSENCE OF ENERGY,
BUT ENERGY / DRIVE IN A DIFFERENT DIRECTION.
WHEN CONSCIOUSLY CHOSEN, RESISTANCE IS HEALTHY.
RESISTANCE SHOULD BE RESPECTED, NOT REGARDED
AS ALIEN AND NEEDING TO BE DESTROYED.
LEARNING CAN BE GAINED FROM RECOGNITION
OF THE POLARITIES IN RESISTANCE.
RESISTANCE SERVES THE FUNCTIONS OF DEFENCE,
PROTECTION, HEALING AND CREATION.
EVERY RESISTANCE IS NECESSARY FOR SELF-REGULATION
AND WITHOUT IT, ORGANIZATIONS AND PEOPLE
CANNOT MAINTAIN THEIR BOUNDARIES.

The journey through the Confusion room is likely to be uncomfortable, but premature closure or conclusions will send you right back into the Denial room. Too much commitment can lead to doing one thing only; too little concern produces aimless wandering. The fear of making a mistake is very strong. The need to protect oneself is so strong that we frequently search for answers before we know what the problem is, and therefore we don't have to suffer the discomfort of the Confusion room. For many of us the temptation of pretence is too strong. The Denial room is not a real room, but many of us pretend it is, and take up permanent residence. However, believe it or not confusion is a state devoutly to be wished, not to be avoided, but it is likely that some support will be required.

Some people and organizations are so keen to avoid the mess of the Confusion room that they build extensions or portacabins to the Denial room, and set up home there. Organizations get really subtle. So terrified are they by the Confusion room that they put in huge programmes like Business Process Re-engineering, Total Quality, Training Needs Assessment etc. and these act as a pseudo-Growth room. One of the reasons these programmes frequently fail is that they never address the issues of the Confusion room, that is, the fears and anxieties about change and loss, both their own and their staff's. So the organization effectively wallpapers over the door to the confusion room, and moves into their castle in the air. They will use lack of time, lack of personnel, poor technology and many other reasons which are usually grounded in reality, so they are plausible. It is the extent to which they are really preventing change that is in each individual's head. *What helps us get through the Confusion room?*

Whenever you start a new anything, expect denial and confusion. Moving yourself into the position where you can see and feel the creativity, is dependent on being able to express the fears and anxieties about the Confusion room. It means having permission to be confused, and not feel that you are supposed to be whole and fully functional immediately following any changes in your life. It means understanding what risk means to you or the people you are trying to support. It means being clear about what you want, and what the change would look like for you. It means knowing what your reality is, and what your expectations might be. It means awareness of yourself and your limitations and the boundaries of other people. It means making and learning from mistakes, something that is terrifying for us. *What will happen if we do it wrong? What will happen if we have got it wrong and therefore respond inappropriately? What will our friends, colleagues and bosses say if we get it wrong? Will we look stupid?*

Giving support without patronizing or devaluing another is difficult for us to do. Receiving help without resisting or feeling in debt or submissive is just as difficult. Experiencing and being aware of these difficulties makes it easier to be on whichever side of the fence we happen to be, but it never makes it easy. Whenever we offer support, there is always a fear that we might be rejected, which seems a real fear when we understand that the individual who accepts help is anxious about being dominated. Many of us will not take the risk of offering or receiving support to avoid these experiences. Learning to give and accept support is a prerequisite for travel through the Confusion room. In a speedy E world, where people have no time to relate and connect, they actually delay not only the ability to change and progress, but also the ability to see ideas and what it would take to make them happen.

Being wrong or potentially "wrong" is key to getting past denial. Entrepreneurs are much happier to do this, maybe because they have a belief in what they want to do, not how they want to do it. Taking up residence in the Denial room can only mean one thing: Denial. Nothing can or will change in the true meaning of the word; it may do on the surface, but there will be no lasting, owned, or excited, change.

Actually embracing error could be a more natural way of learning. If we could give ourselves and others permission to make mistakes, it would reduce the anxiety attached to uncertainty and the stress of being perceived to be out of control. This is the paradox of control: The only way to stay in control is to let go.

Imagine yourself as trying to stay in control by pulling very tightly on a rope, so that it is as taut as can be. Whilst that rope is taut, all your energies are focused on keeping it so, so they cannot be put to any other, more creative use. You cannot see what is coming, because you are focused on the one thing. If you pull too tightly on the rope, it may snap anyway. Also, anyone can come along and cut it while you are so busy holding on.

In the E world, the illusion of working all hours as a means of staying control is illusory. (Surprise!) On the other hand, if you decide when to slacken the rope and when to tighten it, and let go when you choose or think appropriate, you are in control of that rope. The only way to stay in control is to let go. Most of your exciting discoveries about self and others will come while you are in that room. That cannot happen in any other room.

Success in the E world is dependent on your ability to manage in the Confusion room, whether it is yourself or the people you work with. Ideas and solutions that come from the Denial room never happen. They can't, because you haven't accepted that there is a problem, or are solving the wrong problem. Usually you can feel when this is happening; people will say things like, "I've run out of ideas", "It'll never happen", "Well, if that's what you want..."

This learning only takes place through a combination of positive experience and courage and intuitive leaps of faith. We learn to understand ourselves in relationships with others. The more we understand ourselves, the more we understand people. The more we understand people, the more we understand ourselves. This is what is likely to put us and keep us in control, not pushing outrageous goals.

If there is no opportunity to express feelings in connection with the circumstances that elicited them, the feelings will be displaced somewhere else. If feelings are not treated as part of a response or message, or are treated as though they shouldn't be, positive feelings do not get engaged, and the negative feelings cannot be constructively aired and used to choose priorities and alternatives. When feelings are excluded, consciously or unconsciously, commitment, excitement and willingness to risk go out of the window. In extreme cases, the depression that sometimes arises in our irritation at not following our feelings gets projected outward on to the people or circumstances we believe to be responsible for ignoring our feelings. Whatever happens, if feelings are ignored, distrust increases and creativity and learning are inhibited.

"THE MOST TERRIFYING THING IS TO ACCEPT ONESELF COMPLETELY."

[JUNG]

So how long can you stay in the Denial room? Well pretty well permanently if you so desire...we normally do it without knowing or owning up to it. *And what are the consequences of staying in there?* Well, bottom line is that you never really change or grow, with all the feelings that might bring. Actually accepting that you don't want to change, and are going to accept the consequences of that decision is not denial, if you really mean it.

Lurking in the far recesses of the Confusion room is a dimly lit section. You can't get to it unless you have accepted the situation as it is. It is here that you discover the creativity that is necessary to get into the Growth and Renewal room. The creativity and energy come partly from the sense of achievement and awareness that you get from going through the Confusion room. When you reach the curtains, the light goes on...Generating ideas at this point is like falling off a log, and excitement levels are palpable. The wall falls away, and you are in the next room.

Once you have got into the Growth and Renewal room, you don't go back to the Confusion room; the door is one-way. From there it is but a short step to the Contentment room, and in a very short space of time, what was new becomes the old furniture and curtains. Then the whole process starts again. Most of us spend a long time in denial, or we wander through the door into the Confusion room, feel awful and run back into denial. That would be a very normal process. The only door that works both ways is the door between denial and confusion. (That is if you don't board it up...)

Sometimes the things we cling to in our desire to stay safe are the very things that keep us unsafe...the icons of safety become albatrosses around our necks. For many people, survival, safety, security, belonging and recognition are far more important goals than self-fulfilment. If we do not perceive that inventing our own future is going to enable us to feel "safe", or worse, may lose us any of these goals, then there is no way we will enter the Confusion room. *Indeed, why should we?* However, this is a perception, and not necessarily a reality. Unfortunately, the only way we will believe that we are still "safe" is by taking that leap into confusion and experiencing what it really means to us. It's like trusting people. No one will trust anyone because they are told to, or are told they can. ("Trust me, I'm a doctor/accountant/management consultant.....") The only way we learn to trust is by experiencing it. That can take a while, and will inevitably, at some point, involve a leap of faith in something or someone. Inventing your own future means learning to trust yourself.... (courage, faith...).

We sometimes stick to a particular behaviour, because of its familiarity to us. If we know what an outcome will be, no matter how unpleasant it might be, that is sometimes preferable to us than something new, even if there is a chance it might feel good. The unknown seems always less preferable to the known. Some people repeat particularly distressing behaviours from childhood, not because they enjoy them, but because at least they know what will happen to them. This is where a boundary can become either a gateway to the future or a locked and barred door that keeps us trapped.

PRICE OF TIME

Humans outlive machines – it is the human spirit of connection that is crucial for our wellbeing. *What will happen if we lose the spirit of connection? Do you feel you still have it? Do you want it?*

One example of the price of time is a seat on Concorde. *How wonderful is it to leave London at 10 am and arrive in New York at 9 am?* You pay a huge premium for what is a very uncomfortable seat, no movies and a really uptight environment: everyone, including the crew, seems intent on proving how important time is by focusing on work. We are on this flight to work. *Well is that what gaining time means to us? We get to work quicker?* What do we do with the time we have "saved". We do more work.....

Then we start to look out for "time-saving devices", such as bedtime stories condensed by one publisher into literary "quickies" that can be read by a busy parent in only one minute. *And what do those busy parents do with the time they have saved?*

Human beings across the world have several things in common:

WE ARE BORN.

WE LAUGH.

WE CRY.

WE SEEK ACKNOWLEDGEMENT.

WE DIE.

We hardly ever describe those things in those terms; we say that life is too short. Part of the power of the wired world is that it gives us the illusion that we have more time because things are more quickly accessible to us. Whilst that is true, I doubt whether we pause to consider whether that makes us happier or not...Certainly in the very fast high-tech world of Silicon Valley, people make businesses out of freeing up people's time. They do this by providing services from walking your dog to buying and decorating your house. In effect, you turn over your time to someone else; that is time that isn't work-related. So all those leisure activities or things which allow you to get a different perspective on life, or allow you to be in a personal world as opposed to a professional one, are sold to someone else. Even as regards work time; even that can be bartered.

Take Lassobucks.com. This is a website that helps people turn time into money. To use the service, you register and create an "offer" by selecting a category – e.g. accounting or Web design. You describe your skill, the quantity available, the cost per unit, the start time, and the expiration date. If you are invited to join a trading circle (a community organized by location and interest), your offer gets posted. When a member of the circle accepts your offer, your account gets credited with the appropriate number of lassobucks (minus a 5% transaction fee). You can use that currency to buy from others the goods and services that you need to grow your business.

> "'SMALL BUSINESSES AND FREELANCERS HAVE LOTS OF VARIATION IN THEIR SCHEDULES.' SAYS TIMOTHY FONG, 31, FOUNDER OF LASSOBUCKS.COM. 'SOMETIMES THEY'RE INCREDIBLY BUSY, AND OTHER TIMES THEY'RE NOT. WE HELP PEOPLE PUT THEIR EXCESS TIME TO USE.'"
> [ARTICLE IN *FAST COMPANY*]

(How about Lassobucks.com for a name to encapsulate what a culture wants?....)

> "YOUR EXCESS TIME – YOUR UNUSED CAPACITY – IS PERISHABLE."
> [TIMOTHY FONG]

That in itself is an interesting inference. *What does excess time mean? Why does it relate to unused capacity? Is unused capacity work-related? Why does it "perish"? Whatever happened to downtime and time to regenerate and just be?*

There is a difference between using up your time, making the best use of your time, and doing the things that you want to do. If you actually broke down your actions and deeds, what sort of percentage would fall into each of those categories? It's almost as if you can run a life contentment meter on the percentage of time spent on things you want to do. Sometimes if you ask an entrepreneur whether they are doing what they want to do, 90 hours a week, they will loudly shriek YES!

If you ask them whether they are content, that is another story. And entrepreneurs are a very small part of the E world. *How about the vast majority of the E world? How content are you? What difference does it make if you are content or happy?* And I am not talking about some inane Cheshire cat permanent grin (although that might be interesting), but more of those wonderful moments where you feel that your time is yours, you are doing what you want and both your mind and your body let out a long sigh and then you smile... *Do you have time to hold those moments? Do you have them?*

STEALIN' TIME

So buying or exchanging time frees you to do what? It is not so that you can take more vacation, it's usually so that you can spend more time at work. Those consultancies that will do everything for the busy executive have your time. All so that an individual can put more time and energy into work. *Is that technologically driven?* Technology itself cannot make you do anything. The wired world does not force you to make decisions. It might put different choices your way, but it doesn't take away the choice, unless you let it. Choice about how you spend your time is maybe at the heart of identifying what is important to you and how that affects your connections and relationships.

> CHOICES...
>
> TO REMEMBER OR FORGET;
> TO DO OR NOT TO DO;
> TO BE OR NOT TO BE.

How important are other people in your choice process? And therefore how do your relationships impact on your choices? Of course if you have no time for relationships, *does that mean you have vested all your choice mechanisms in self? Do we actually have the control over events such that we can afford to ignore others in pursuit of our goals? Do you?*

> "MY FAMILY IS HEALTHY, HAPPY AND SMART, BUT TIME IS ALL WE HAVE ON THIS PLANET, AND MONEY IS MEANINGLESS. I'M SPENDING THE ONLY ASSET THAT MATTERS, MY TIME, AND A LOT OF IT, ON THE COMPANY AND GROWTH. I WISH I COULD CLONE MYSELF....NO ONE CAN SUSTAIN THE HYPERGROWTH STATUS AS CEO FOR MANY YEARS. THE INTERNET IS A SELF FULFILLING, CAREER LIMITING DEVICE."
> **[MARK WALSH, 45-YEAR-OLD CEO OF VERTICALNET IN AN INTERVIEW IN THE *INDUSTRY STANDARD*]**

Some do decide to stop working and then feel left out of what is going on. They seem scared they are going to miss something; but when you ask what the something is, they don't know. Some of the new millionaires are comfortable with not working, and these are people who would have been comfortable with themselves and not working before they had money. Money does not change the fundamentals of who you are; you still have the problems and qualities you had to begin with, except for the financial ones.

The interesting thing about many of the people working 80-hour weeks in start-ups in Silicon Valley is that they actually enjoy their jobs, and are not working for some faceless boss somewhere. They may not be happy about working those hours, but they feel it is out of choice. What is fascinating is what happens when they have their IPO and make their money, and they can quit working. Very few of them leave to sail around the world or retire to the mountains. *Why? Is it a pathological need to maybe go one better? Is it an addiction? Is it just because they love working?* Each of these would have a different impact on relationships.

They also seem to find it hard to distinguish their work from their jobs...their work belongs to them, and their jobs belong to their organization (even if the organization belongs to them). If you are your job, you lose you, and your time is spent on someone else without time for you. To stay grounded in any world, it is important to know what your work is: that is your identity, that which you alone contribute.

RICHARD "WHAT SHOULD I DO NOW?"

MARK "I DON'T KNOW, SOMETHING GREAT."

[OVERHEARD CONVERSATION BETWEEN TWO ENTREPRENEURS]

"I WAS BORN TO WEB."

[20-SOMETHING IN A TV ADVERT]

"I WAS BORN TO BE AN INTERNET JUNKIE."

[10-YEAR-OLD IN SAME TV ADVERT]

SEVEN AGES OF MAN

So much of our need for relationships is grounded in what is happening in our lives, and various life events. They can totally throw plans and ambitions out of synch. *When you have no contingency time to flex with life events, what happens?*

Jill was a software designer with an international software house. Highly ambitious, she ran with all the company's punishing and unreal schedules. She worked all her weekends and for one year took no holiday. It was not a logistical challenge for her, as she did not have a relationship or family to consider, just herself. The sacrifices she felt she had made led her to be less sympathetic with those on her team who did have commitments outside the project. She became less and less respected by the team, who ended up doing the bare minimum; usually resentfully. She then started to lose team members. This just made her throw herself more and more into her work, and take more on herself. After a company health screening, she was sent for further clinical tests, and was diagnosed with cervical cancer. Initially she tried to continue on as if nothing had happened, and this was just another glitch in the project she had to find a way around. Her denial led to a much longer recovery period, followed by an enforced absence from work, on company doctor's orders. When she still didn't recover, and she had to undergo more tests, something gave way inside her. She was trying to hold together herself and the job at a moment in time when she really needed to be focusing on herself. She had put her value for time above herself. She was also terrified of being alone, and had isolated herself so far from friends and work colleagues that her worst fears were realized. She was facing personal crisis on her own. Her work schedule had left no time for contingency; for an unexpected event.

Our motivation and drive can be very heavily influenced by external events, and the way we perceive work and relationships.

So much has been written about changes in our attitudes to time and relationships – since Shakespeare's time. What follows is a summarized tale of recognized, thorough and authoritative thought and research. It is intended to provoke thought, not provide a definitive "answer". Investigate.....

We all have developmental stages we go through; some go through them faster than others, other people get stuck at different stages...take a look through and see which time of your life you think you are in. The columns relate to motivational needs: the higher the column, the stronger the need. Of course, if one column goes high, another column will be pushed down.... If you want to impact on someone, you need to understand their need, rather than try and influence them with your needs. As human beings we are awfully good at projecting our needs on to others, then wonder why they are not persuaded by our arguments.

Column A: Material Comfort

This is about a need for survival: what does my body need today? This is largely about money; not money for the Porsche or the country cottage, but money to feed and clothe you and your family. Because this is such a primal need, it also measures a desire to avoid stress. When your whole life is threatened by lack of food, for example, it is unusual for people to want to take on responsibility for anything other than finding food. It is very heavily affected by external circumstances: anything that raises your need for money such as loss of job, moving home, putting a new bathroom in, even going on an expensive holiday or spending spree will raise this need. Everyone in the E world gets affected by this at some time or other. It's worth remembering that if this is high, it will suppress something else that might usually be high.

Column B: Structure

This is about what my body needs tomorrow. This is about safety, security and frameworks. It measures your need to "know where you be". Some folk have a permanently high need for structures in their lives, others low. Entrepreneurs usually have a low need, but successful entrepreneurs always travel in twos, and behind the visionary frontperson is a structure person who sweeps up and checks after the entrepreneur (Anita Roddick and her husband, Lords Hanson and White, Richard Branson). People with a very low structure need can get intensely frustrated when they have to influence someone with a high need and vice versa. Low-structure people usually get bored very quickly so need a 15-second high-concept story, or you have lost them. High-structure people need detail and proof, and like to ask lots of questions. Very high-structure people have to see things in advance....

In times of change, people's structure need rises and they may require more frameworks than they might at other times. High structure is also associated with risk aversion; so in a time of change, people's structure need is up, they are more risk averse, and what is it you really want them to do? Take risks of course..... The only way they will is if they can see some framework to it. They also need more communication than normal; unfortunately, in a time of change, most people and organizations clam up. Even letting people know that you don't know is helpful.

Many E companies are low-structure, and this is rarely a problem in the beginning. Sometimes, things don't get followed through, or when the company moves from its start-up phase to its consolidation phase and has no people to do routine work and consolidate ideas and processes, the company fails.

Column C: Relationships

This column does not measure people's need to have illicit relationships although it might do...It measures a need to belong, to be part of something, to be identified with a group. This column does not measure skill levels; you can have a huge need to belong, and have the interpersonal skills of a rhino. Alternatively, you can have a low relationship need and very good interpersonal skills. If your need is high, it is crucially important to you to be seen as part of a group. It would be difficult for you to work in isolation. You are likely to enjoy an open plan office where you can wander around and chat at someone's desk. The worst thing that could happen to you would be to put you on a project on your own. Just out of interest, the English seem to have one of the lowest relationship needs in the world. (Must be that island mentality, or possibly why we like being in charge of things, but don't like belonging.) For people in a fast-paced E world, not having this need met might leave people stressed and depressed, particularly if they felt they were letting other people down.

Column D: Recognition

This column measures how strong your need is to be recognized and valued. All humans want to be recognized and appreciated; the trick is knowing what recognition would look like for each individual. For some it is found in the trappings of achievement, like the fast car, house or designer clothing. For others, it is as simple as a hello in the corridor. Those with a bottomless pit of recognition show it very blatantly, by seeking either limelight or feedback constantly. It's easy to feed this need; you just give people the recognition they want....

Column E: Power

This is about a need to control and influence. Sometimes those with a high control need find it hard to delegate and to ask questions, and if this is coupled with a high structure need, can be both bureaucratic and autocratic...(not too helpful for the fast changes of the E world). Most managers in corporations have a high need for control, otherwise why would they want to manage? It isn't a negative to have a high control need; it's whether an inappropriate need affects your ability to impact on a situation.

Column F: Self-fulfilment

This is the "do your own thing" column and breaks down into three subheadings: a need for autonomy, to do things your own way, in your own time without anyone looking over your shoulder; a need for creativity and innovation, always to be doing something new, whether it's designing a new program or redoing the filing system; and a need for personal growth, a need to be forever learning. These three things are very present in the self-employed, designers, researchers and software developers. Information technology professionals tend to score highly on this column. This is the entrepreneur's column. Most large corporations are not very good at motivating this particular need. It is certainly the driver behind most successful new and exciting E businesses. If this is the only driver, the business does not survive, as personal drive and ideas alone do not an economically viable business make. Clive Sinclair's "ideocracy" would be a good example, where there was no shortage of ideas and intelligence, but no one wanted to do anything once they had the ideas......

So these profiles ebb and flow, depending on what is happening in our environment. Then they tend to follow this "seven ages" cycle; but how long that will remain so, who knows. The ages seem to be found in most cultures, as they correspond to both physiological and psychological development cycles. The differences appear in different cultures' attitudes to the behaviours.

"HIS ACTS BEING SEVEN AGES..."

THE THINGS THAT ARE IMPORTANT TO US
VARY AT DIFFERENT POINTS IN OUR HUMAN LIFECYCLE
WITH APOLOGIES TO SHAKESPEARE
FOR NOT STICKING PRECISELY TO HIS

1

"AT FIRST, THE INFANT,
MEWLING AND PUKING
IN THE NURSE'S ARMS ..."

AGE 0 – 10

Little is known about motivation profiles in the early years. It is not clear how much influence hereditary factors have in determining future profiles. What is clear is that environmental influences do have a major effect. Eldest children have higher concerns for structure, partly because they are the children of amateur parents, and partly because they are left in charge of their younger siblings, coming to rely on rules to maintain order ("Mummy said you mustn't ...").

Achievement-oriented parents "teach" achievement orientation in their children, both by example and by setting goals, giving praise or rewards. Many schools use the same pressures to the same ends, especially fee-paying schools selected by the parents.

How will this age group, brought up in an E world, differ and respond to their parents? Certainly, the age limits for this developmental stage are getting lower, i.e. children are moving faster.

2

"AND THEN THE WHINING SCHOOLBOY,
WITH HIS SATCHEL AND SHINING
MORNING FACE, CREEPING LIKE SNAIL
UNWILLINGLY TO SCHOOL ..."

AGE 10 – 14

By the early teens, the underlying trained-in profile emerges as stable for the first time. The average profile for the achievement-oriented population is:

A: MATERIAL COMFORT B: STRUCTURE C: RELATIONSHIPS
D: RECOGNITION E: POWER F: SELF FULFILLMENT

Whatever the underlying profile, it will now be exposed to a series of relatively predictable changes, reflecting relatively predictable changes in the social environment. These distortions are illustrated in the next paragraphs as they affect the average profile. Yes, we hit a high achievement spot, which usually doesn't last very long.

3

"AND THEN THE LOVER,
SIGHING LIKE FURNACE,
WITH A WOEFUL BALLAD
MADE TO HIS
MISTRESS' EYEBROW ..."

AGE 14 – 23

Adolescence. Physiological changes and the social pressure to form relationships with the opposite sex are strongly reflected: concerns for material comfort and relationships increase. Achievement drives become less important:

A: MATERIAL COMFORT B: STRUCTURE C: RELATIONSHIPS
D: RECOGNITION E: POWER F: SELF FULFILLMENT

What is the most important thing to you when you are in your teens? Pretty much sex, drugs and rock and roll....online or not......Ironically, it is during this period that society asks the individual to decide on a career. It is not surprising that two-thirds of graduates over the age of 35 report that they chose the wrong degree subject at university. At least the E world has presented opportunities that don't frame one course of action.

The duration and age at onset of adolescence vary widely between individuals. It is usually complete by the early twenties, but may be delayed even further. If the individual has not resolved these issues by about 27 or 28, it is likely that he or she will remain psychologically immature.

4

"THEN A SOLDIER, FULL OF STRANGE OATHS
AND BEARDED LIKE THE PARD, JEALOUS
IN HONOUR, SUDDEN AND QUICK IN QUARREL,
SEEKING THE BUBBLE REPUTATION
EVEN IN THE CANNON'S MOUTH ..."

AGE 23 – 38

After the upsets of adolescence, the underlying profile re-emerges as the individual resolves the questions of identity and relationships posed by becoming adult. Achievement orientation will increase in this age range, reaching a peak in the early to middle thirties:

A: MATERIAL COMFORT B: STRUCTURE C: RELATIONSHIPS
D: RECOGNITION E: POWER F: SELF FULFILLMENT

This achievement orientation, however, is exposed to two distortions:

179

Mating

For both men and women, if the individual has not formed a stable pair bond with a partner, the concern for relationships rises dramatically in the late twenties:

A: MATERIAL COMFORT B: STRUCTURE C: RELATIONSHIPS
D: RECOGNITION E: POWER F: SELF FULFILLMENT

This may be partly instinctive (the "mating instinct"), but social pressures are likely to be more significant as the individual is increasingly out of step with his or her peers. For those who nevertheless remain unpaired, this concern will gradually die back to the trained-in level, as he or she becomes reconciled to remaining solo.

First Child

The birth of the first child presents a dramatic moment in the family, and this shows up in the motivation profile of the father. Material comfort, structure and security, and relationships are all exposed to change, and become dominant. Achievement concerns become less significant:

A: MATERIAL COMFORT B: STRUCTURE C: RELATIONSHIPS
D: RECOGNITION E: POWER F: SELF FULFILLMENT

This profile is similar to that found amongst shop-floor operators. For some 9 to 18 months, the high-achieving male becomes, motivationally, a process worker.

There is wide variation in both the duration and onset of this fascination with home events. Some organizations over-react to the man's loss of "motivation" – foolishly, for the career motivation will return more strongly than before. Subsequent children, however, have no noticeable impact on the father's career motivation.

During the thirties, the achievement drives become more and more significant. The individual is now fully experienced in his or her functional role, and reaching that level within the organization at which career opportunities become more and more restricted. There is very little evidence that these basic principles have been dramatically changed by E world events, although women seem to be having children later, and men seem to be playing a larger part in that process.

5

THE MID-CAREER DECISION POINT.
AGE 38 – 45

Many managers at this level of restricted opportunity are satisfied with their achievement. Usually, some 50% are realistic and comfortable with their attainment. Others, typically some 10%, will continue to be promoted and to find an outlet for their achievement concerns – they will continue to channel their energies mainly into their careers until retirement. But the balance, almost 40% of (usually) male managers in large organizations, become blocked in their careers, and this shows up in their profiles.

This is also the age, unfortunately, at which the individual's body starts to show irreversible signs of middle age – and the individual's concern for their body increases. Concern for structure fades – they feel trapped in the structure which has become a cage rather than a ladder to be climbed. Achievement drives, frustrated, die away:

A: MATERIAL COMFORT B: STRUCTURE C: RELATIONSHIPS
D: RECOGNITION E: POWER F: SELF FULFILLMENT

The high-achieving male has returned, motivationally, to adolescence, and exhibits many adolescent behaviours. Drug abuse, sexual fantasy, feelings of acute depression and identity crises all increase. Suicide rates increase, peculiar career decisions abound, and many marriages fail as the man seeks to rediscover his self-respect in sexual adventure.

The majority will recover within two years, emerging with a realistic view of their attainments. Most people go through this in some shape or form; sometimes, the searching involves buying a motor bike, changing a job, going travelling, taking up a hobby; other times it could be destructive to the individual. A few never recover, remaining disillusioned and unreconciled to their situation. It is probable that many of these will die before the age of 50. (The data that John Hunt has suggests that women go through a mid-life crisis at different points; usually around age 30, with a baby or career decision; or if they have children, when the children no longer need their mother. In both cases, the motivational profile is almost the reverse of the adolescent one: high on self-fulfilment and recognition.)

Organizations largely create this problem, by their structure and by the creation and maintenance of unrealistic career aspirations. There is little that can be done to help the individual, other than support and patience.

6

"AND THEN THE JUSTICE, IN FAIR ROUND BELLY
WITH GOOD CAPON LINED, WITH EYES SEVERE, AND BEARD
OF FORMAL CUT, FULL OF WISE SAWS AND
MODERN INSTANCES; AND SO HE PLAYS HIS PART ..."

AGE 45 – 55

The golden age for many. The marriage, if it has survived any mid-career crisis, will be re-negotiated as the children leave home, emerging on a sounder footing as a result. With children financially independent, and with many wives resuming their careers, increased resources are available to meet fewer demands. The achievement concerns continue, or recover from mid-career depression, but the concern for relationships increases to match their level.

This is a sound group of workers who have a balance between home and work, know what they want from life and are frequently experienced and knowledgeable about their work. Many companies make these people redundant, as they feel that young blood will move the company faster. In the E world, many of this age group are being sought out by the young entrepreneurs as advisers or mentors to their start-ups. These companies use the calmness, rationality and detached objectivity of these people to counterpoint their pace and impatience.

This profile is also beginning to shift. As many organizations make people redundant, they are forcing people into job decisions they might not have made themselves. Many people take up new careers, doing things they have always wanted to do, but couldn't face the risk. At the start of that new journey, you often see a return to the high-achieving profile.

We can now see the start of a process that continues almost uninterrupted until death – the gradual flattening of the profile as concerns for body and security increase relative to achievement:

A: MATERIAL COMFORT B: STRUCTURE C: RELATIONSHIPS
D: RECOGNITION E: POWER F: SELF FULFILLMENT

Retirement

Many managers continue to invest most of their achievement concerns into work. For them, retirement presents a crisis – overnight, the outlet for their achievements for the last 40 years is cut off. Achievement concerns, frustrated, collapse. The high achiever is pushed into the motivational profile of the process worker:

A: MATERIAL COMFORT B: STRUCTURE C: RELATIONSHIPS
D: RECOGNITION E: POWER F: SELF FULFILLMENT

Life loses its meaning. Psychological collapse is followed for many by physical collapse. In some organizations, almost a quarter of their managers will die within one year of retirement.

7

"THE SIXTH AGE SHIFTS INTO THE LEAN AND SLIPPER'D PANTALOON,
WITH SPECTACLES ON NOSE AND POUCH ON SIDE,
HIS YOUTHFUL HOSE WELL SAVED, A WORLD TOO WIDE FOR HIS SHRUNK SHANK,
AND HIS BIG MANLY VOICE, TURNING AGAIN TOWARD CHILDISH TREBLE,
PIPES AND WHISTLES IN HIS SOUND ..."

AGE 60/65 – ?

For those who succeed in developing ways to express their achievement concerns
outside of work, retirement presents no crisis. Many organizations provide pre-
retirement training, but this is usually focused on financial planning. In any case, it
starts too late for any meaningful redirection of achievement. The individual needs time
to become involved – a year is not enough. The gradual increase in body and security
concerns continues:

A: MATERIAL COMFORT B: STRUCTURE C: RELATIONSHIPS
D: RECOGNITION E: POWER F: SELF FULFILLMENT

"LAST SCENE OF ALL, THAT ENDS THIS STRANGE EVENTFUL HISTORY,
IS SECOND CHILDISHNESS AND MERE OBLIVION,
SANS TEETH, SANS EYES, SANS TASTE, SANS EVERYTHING."

AGE ? – DEATH

With increasing age, the motivation profile becomes dominated by the basic survival concerns. And, with increasing barriers to achievement, the achievement concerns die down:

A: MATERIAL COMFORT B: STRUCTURE C: RELATIONSHIPS
D: RECOGNITION E: POWER F: SELF FULFILLMENT

With acknowledgement to John Hunt (*Managing People at Work*, McGraw Hill 1986) and John Harter, and apologies to William Shakespeare (*As You Like It*, II.vii.143–166).

In terms of the E world, the major protagonists are in the high-achieving phase, but many of the people they have to deal with are not. Also the customer is in many different phases of their cycle, and therefore their needs are different. When people are at different stages in their cycle, their need to relate to others is very different. Some of this gets played out in generational gaps. In his book *The Clock of the Long Now*, Stewart Brand suggests there are several layers to civilization, which all vibrate at their own speed frequency:

→ FASHION
→ COMMERCE
→ INFRASTRUCTURE
→ GOVERNANCE
→ CULTURE
→ NATURE

He suggests that these different layers have different speeds and are connected to the human lifecycle; for example, adolescents are fascinated by fashion and its now now now, whereas older people are bored by it and more interested in culture. The E world seems to resonate much more loudly at the fashion and commerce levels, and less strongly as you go down the list. *If the E world is to fully develop as a civilization, does that mean it has to find a way to resonate at all levels? Does it need to fully develop as a civilization?*

TIME OF YOUR LIFE
There have always been and probably always will be generational gaps in thinking as society and social evolution change people's experience and expectations. In terms of the E world, there does seem to be a difference in the way different generations approach this way of being.

The Net Generation or "N"generation, as described by Don Tapscott in his book *Growing up Digital*, are a reality. *What makes this generation?* It is the first generation to grow up at most surrounded, at least touched in some way, by digital media. Computers are as much a part of their life as television was to the baby boomers. One of the big differences between the Ngeners and the Genxers is that the Genxers were still exploring and defining the digital world. The Ngeners take it for granted and are moving on from there. For that reason, it seems that the communication gap between these two groups may be even bigger than that between the baby boomers and the Genxers.

Every generation has difficulty with communicating with those who came before and after. One of the interesting observations about the Ngeners is that they seem to have more in common with the baby boomers than the Genxers.

Their parents by and large have given them more; in terms of both time and material access. They have a far more positive outlook on the world, whereas the Genxers carry with them the scars of transition and behave accordingly. For the first time children are more knowledgeable and comfortable than their parents, educators and corporate employers about an innovation central to society.

Few parents know what their children are doing in Cyberspace, and don't know how to ask. Well, there's nothing new in that … a child's world is usually off limits to a parent. "What did you do at school today?" "Oh nothing much." Usually as soon as they start school, they see their time as their own. With the advent of computers in many homes, they spend time earlier either on their own playing games or even in the chat rooms. They are learning with an interactive medium to make relationships of the kind that children love: they can turn them on and off whenever they like, and even adjust how fast or slow they go.

I wonder what that will do to their concept of time and what is doable, or can be expected. Put the ease with which children take to interactive media together with parents who are working and very wrapped up in their work, and you get a different sense of time in the E family. The difference is how much independence they have to navigate their world with all the data available to them. *How do they know what is "true"? Do they have the skills to create and relate? Do they understand the consequences of their actions? How do they make their decisions? What are the social, commercial and political implications of a group of young people so much more clued up than those in legitimate power? What will these people do with their knowledge? What contracts do they make with the world and their workplace?* Many observe that they come to work very willing but with the rewards up front; they have a sense of entitlement, and are not ready to "pay their dues".

Ron Zemke, Claire Raines and Bob Filipczak described four different generational groups that come together in the workplace. (WARNING!! These are generalizations, and should be treated as such.)Thinking about the differences and putting meaning behind some widely used categories may help to explain some of the relationship issues.

Veterans (1922–1943) Born between two major defining events of the 20th century: the Great Depression and World War 2. They see themselves as the repository for history and wisdom. They find it hard to learn from "wired" 20-year-olds, and are rarely comfortable unless their experience is valued and openly acknowledged. They appreciate logic, discipline and tradition. They are not fond of stories or examples that are personal.

Baby Boomers (1943–1960) These are the post-war babies, who are passionate about bringing heart and humanity to the office, and creating a fair and level playing field for all. They want to change things and turn them around. They also have a passion for non-authoritarian learning; i.e. you can't tell them what to do, they prefer to find out for themselves. (There is a Boomer Institute in Cleveland Ohio.....) They are the biggest market for self-help media, and tend to be optimistic, and are attracted to the concept of working in groups.

> "...TOXIC LEVELS OF SELF INVOLVEMENT HAVE BEEN DISCOVERED IN NEARLY 80 PER CENT OF CHILDREN BORN IN THE POST WAR BABY BOOM. THE ARTICLE'S FINDINGS WERE BASED ON BLOOD SAMPLES TAKEN FROM 25,000 BABIES BORN BETWEEN 1945 AND 1948, WHOSE BLOOD CONTAINED DANGEROUSLY HIGH LEVELS OF SELF-INVOLVEMENT, SOME 40 TIMES HIGHER THAN THOSE OF AMERICANS BORN IN THE PREVIOUS GENERATION......IT IS ENTIRELY PLAUSIBLE THAT BY 1970, THE VAST MAJORITY OF AMERICANS WILL EXHIBIT STRANGE SYMPTOMS INCLUDING ABNORMALLY HIGH INTEREST IN THEIR OWN SATISFACTION, A PREOCCUPATION WITH SELF ACTUALISATION, AND AN EERIE LACK OF BLIND FAITH IN THEIR ELECTED OFFICIALS, CLERGY AND PEERS."
>
> [*THE ONION*]

Genxers (1961–1980) They are comfortable with change, but want to be the ones who create and direct the change. They have their own orientation to time and space, believing that it is not important how and when the job gets done, as long as it gets done. They have little respect for authority, just because of the number of stripes you have, but they do respect people who can demonstrate that they "know their stuff". They see themselves as free agents, and put having fun pretty close to the top of their work priorities.

Nexters (1980–present) The oldest Nexters are starting jobs. They seem to be a composite group with the technology savvy of the Genxers, the can-do attitude of the Veterans and the "groupy" stuff of the Boomers. For them, technology is as natural as air.

They don't think of it as being anything other than standard.
They have grown up with it, in a similar way to the later Boomers growing up with television. Interestingly they seem less anarchistic than Genxers. In fact it may well be that they have more trouble communicating with Genxers. They also seem to resonate with Veterans.

The Genxers are the group most people associate with E commerce. They have technology at their heart and they were the generation who were very present and instrumental in creating the pace and nature of the E world. However, they seem to find it hard to relate to the group coming up after them.

Genxers made no contracts and wanted to hit back at a world that had abandoned them. This is a generation that was promised the world by their parents, the Boomers who had fought for love, peace, and sexual and professional freedom. Unfortunately, what happened was that the promised loving, stable family frequently ended in divorce, or with a latch-key childhood. Jobs were hard to come by, and they had to work really hard to get anywhere. And as for sexual freedom, well along came AIDS...What very simplistically the Genxers were given was a heap of broken promises. Not surprisingly, they felt abandoned, alienated and let down. They were very unlikely to trust authority. They felt that the only people they could trust were themselves; that was one thing they had learned to do. Everything from their music to their dress became a gesture of independence and "We can do it without you." Well, they did make contracts, but with themselves. Technology appeared at a time that allowed them to claim a field as their own. They may even have embraced technology more fervently than they might have done, as it gave them a lever of power over those in authority. It also gave them independence and a connection that couldn't abandon them.

They describe themselves as worshipping at the altar of Authenticity. The only thing that they will hold as a non-negotiable is being true to themselves. This often translates as focused, self-centred and selfish. Certainly many of the Boomers see them as ungrateful; as having taken the legacy that they worked so hard to provide, and using it to further their individual needs, as opposed to the greater good. Genxers will reply that they are very interested in their own communities, and they would prefer to get on and do something about it rather than wave placards.

"...THE REALITY BITES VISION OF OUR GENERATION AS AN AIMLESS-SLACKER, ANGST-RIDDEN KIND OF AFFAIR WAS SOMETHING THAT NONE OF US EVER REALLY RELATED TO. AND IT SEEMED A DISDAINFUL OVER-SIMPLIFICATION THAT WAS BEING FED TO US BY THE BABY-BOOMER GENERATION THAT ON MOST LEVELS UNDERESTIMATED THE DEPTH OF THE CYNICISM AND PARALYSIS AND DESPAIR AT THE HEART OF THE MAJORITY OF PEOPLE IN OUR AGE GROUP."

[ED NORTON IN AN INTERVIEW]

THINKING BEYOND THE WAVE

Genxers don't let lack of experience limit what they will do or try to do; 45-year-old managers' experience limits them, in that they often think about what they know rather than what they don't know, and therefore end up in the same place with the same solutions. Sometimes the way that gets played out in the E world is that companies want to change, but they look for structural and operational changes rather than the "wow". In time terms, the technology wave comes over very fast, and before it's over, the next one is approaching. It isn't about turning back the waves, nor is it even riding them, because that might get you into shore, and by the time you've picked up your surfboard, another wave has come and knocked you over. It's being ahead of the wave, and knowing that to make sure you survive beyond the next wave, you need positive relationships that stop you going under while you prepare and move on to the next one. Then, you can actually enjoy the ride, and even while you are enjoying it, come up with new ways to ride the next one. If, however, your only concern is to survive the wave, that is all you will do.

Most people have more of a say in what happens to them through technology; but few have the understanding of how to get the most out of it.

As I was writing this book four themes kept re-occurring..., illusion, fantasy, control and choice. The wired world offers us plenty of all of these. So does and did the unwired world. *What are the differences in the offer? Or are there no differences in the offer, just in the way we respond? What is real and what is fantasy?*

My guess is we need them both. We need to be able to know which is which and adjust expectation and response levels accordingly. *How do we allocate our time in those different worlds? Do we even know we are there?* Of course we confuse them. Actually knowing the difference may be the key to getting the best out of any world, wired or otherwise. *How do you spend your time in those different worlds?*

"IT ABSOLUTELY NEEDS INTERACTIVITY," KEVIN KELLEY SUGGESTS. "ONLY HALF OF WHAT PEOPLE WANT TO DO IS BE DRIVEN. THE WEB IS ABOUT A COHERENT, LIQUID WAY TO ADD OTHER DIMENSIONS TO OUR LIVES. WE WANT TO TALK MANY-TO-MANY LIKE IN CHATROOMS, AND HAVE PEER CONVERSATIONS TAILORED TO OURSELVES. WE WANT TO BE ABLE TO DRIVE. WHAT WE WANT IS WELL-ROUNDED MEDIA THAT DOES BOTH. IT WILL DRIVE WHEN WE DON'T FEEL LIKE DRIVING, BUT WILL ALSO GIVE US THE POWER TO TALK TO OUR FRIENDS, TALK BACK, CUSTOMIZE THE MESSAGE AND INVITE ADVERTISERS IN IF THEY HAVE SOMETHING WE CARE ABOUT. IT'S NOT ABOUT OLD VERSUS NEW MEDIA, BUT ABOUT COMPLETE MEDIA, FULL MEDIA."

He was referring to the AOL/Time Warner deal, announced in January 2000. It is worth noting that Ted Turner, one of the chief architects of the deal, and vice-chairman of the new company, said of the deal, "The excitement with which I did that matched the excitement I had 42 years or so ago, when I first made love." This may be a clue to the relationships that are meaningful to this person.

In this so called customer-oriented world, how many times have you been put on hold, passed from one digitized number-choice program to another, and/or been forced to spend your valuable time listening to muzak or sales talk? Unless you have an IT department, you may even have been on the receiving end of Microsoft's technical helpline in the US. They have so many calls that they hired a live DJ who is running a live music programme while you are waiting. They obviously feel that their money is best spent on passing your time listening to the DJ's choice of music rather than spending the money on more people to respond to your queries. *Following on that train of thought, if your perceived time does become so precious how do you make it count? Do you spend it on building relationships? Do you spend it accumulating? Do you spend more time with Amazon.com than you do with your friends?*

There is as much danger in polarizing work and pleasure in as there is the blurring of work and pleasure that exists in the E world, where it seems hard for people to work out what they want from their time and go find it. It may well be that this is the evil of choice that technology and other sophistications have brought us, when really we were much happier when we were told that you come into work at 9 am. and you leave at 5 pm, and your weekends are free.

It seems that like everything we have to deal with in life, we have to make conscious choices about how to spend our time and who to spend it with. Enjoying your work does not mean it is all-consuming. Very few people on their deathbeds regret not having spent more time at work; many regret not spending time with people they care about, doing things they really wanted to do.

If we can perhaps see time as the real genetic code of man, our other experiences
of pace, space and depth are the outcome of the interaction between our time and our
environment (environment in the widest sense so including the one we create in our
own minds).

If we are an evolving species, then our understanding and use of time may be the
constancy factor that helps us grow and evolve. *If we have our pace, space or depth moved too
far out so there is no time to test and filter, what will happen to our development?*

"WE HAD THE EXPERIENCE
BUT MISSED THE MEANING."

[T.S. ELIOT]

[END]

"WE NEED OPPORTUNITIES NOW, NOT EFFICIENCIES. WE NEED INSPIRED IMPROVISATION,
NOT SOLUTIONS. TECHNOLOGY CAN NO LONGER BIND US IN A VAST TONNAGE OF IRON, BARBED WIRE
AND BRICK. WE WILL STOP HEAVING BULKY MACHINES UPHILL. INSTEAD, WE BEGIN JUDGING
ENTIRE TECHNO-COMPLEXES AS THEY VIRTUALLY UNFOLD, JUDGING THEM BY STANDARDS THAT ARE,
IN SOME VERY BASIC SENSE, AESTHETIC.

THIS IS THE TIME TO BE THOUGHTFUL, BE EXPRESSIVE, BE GENEROUS, BE "TAKEN ADVANTAGE OF."
THE CHANNELS EXIST NOW TO GIVE CREATIVITY AWAY, AT NO COST, TO MILLIONS.
NEVER MIND IF YOU MAKE LARGE SUMS OF MONEY ALONG THE WAY. IF YOU SUCCESSFULLY
SEIZE ATTENTION, NOTHING IS MORE LIKELY. IN A START-UP SOCIETY, HUGE SUMS CAN FALL ON INNOCENT
PARTIES, ALMOST BY ACCIDENT. THAT CANNOT BE HELPED, SO DON'T WORRY ABOUT IT ANY MORE.
HENCEFORTH, ARTISTIC INTEGRITY SHOULD BE JUDGED, NOT BY ONE'S CLASSIC BOHEMIAN SECLUSION
FROM SATANIC MILLS AND THE GRASPING BOURGEOISIE, BUT BY WHAT ONE CREATES AND GIVES AWAY.
THAT IS THE ONLY SCALE OF NONCOMMERCIAL INTEGRITY THAT MAKES ANY SENSE NOW."

[BRUCE STERLING]

Technology is changing faster than markets, markets are changing faster than
customers, customers are changing faster than organizations, and organizations are
changing faster than the people who run them.

Catch up...........With Yourself

E BUSINESS
O BUSINESS (OPTICAL)
M BUSINESS (MOBILE)

We seem to be hurtling towards a world where people are permanently connected to
the Internet in some shape or form. *Who knows what else will be around by the time this book
is published?*..... There is no shortage of business ideas; just a need for people who can
make them work. That has not changed, and is unlikely to change.

The E world and our relationships with each other. There are clearly things changing
in our universe, but our needs as humans remain pretty much the same. There is no
malevolent force pushing us into this situation. We have created it ourselves. The ultimate
independence. *Can we deal with it?*

"NO ONE KNOWS

ANYTHING."

[WILLIAM GOLDMAN, *ADVENTURES IN THE SCREEN TRADE*]

"HOPE IS AN ORIENTATION OF THE SPIRIT, AN ORIENTATION OF THE HEART; IT TRANSCENDS THE WORLD THAT IS IMMEDIATELY EXPERIENCED AND IS ANCHORED SOMEWHERE BEYOND ITS HORIZONS. HOPE IS DEFINITELY NOT THE SAME THING AS OPTIMISM. IT IS NOT THE CONVICTION THAT SOMETHING WILL TURN OUT WELL, BUT THE CERTAINTY THAT SOMETHING MAKES SENSE, REGARDLESS OF HOW IT TURNS OUT.

IN SHORT, I THINK THAT THE DEEPEST AND MOST IMPORTANT FORM OF HOPE IS SOMETHING WE GET FROM ELSEWHERE. IT IS ALSO THIS HOPE, ABOVE ALL, WHICH GIVES US THE STRENGTH TO LIVE AND CONTINUOUSLY TRY NEW THINGS."

[VACLAV HAVEL, *DISTURBING THE PEACE*]

The day before the deadline for this book, I received a phone call at one o'clock in the morning California time, from Thailand. It was someone calling to tell me that my daughter had been seriously injured in an accident. That same morning, I travelled half way around the world to see her. The thing that kept both myself and my daughter going was my contact with friends and family around the world, at all times of the day, through email.

The practical and emotional support was incredible and was constant over a two-week period. It would have been hard for people to offer their thoughts and support to the same level in another way partly because of the distance and the time zone difference. It also allowed people who would have felt uncomfortable speaking ear to ear to offer something in their own way.

The E world provided a means of maintaining and strengthening relationships that would not have been possible any other way.

[INDEX]